1993

D0252689

Songbirds,
Truffles,
and Wolves

ALSO BY GARY PAUL NABHAN

The Desert Smells Like Rain
Gathering the Desert
Enduring Seeds

Songbirds, Truffles, and Wolves

An American Naturalist in Italy

Gary Paul Nabhan

PANTHEON BOOKS
NEW YORK AND SAN FRANCISCO

Copyright © 1993 by Gary Nabhan

All rights reserved under International and Pan-American Copyright Conventions. Published in the United States by Pantheon Books, a division of Random House, Inc., New York, and simultaneously in Canada by Random House of Canada Limited, Toronto.

Grateful acknowledgment is made to the following for permission to reprint previously published material:

National Gardening Association: Excerpt from "Lost Heritage" by Lorraine Lilja from the January/February 1981 issue of *Gardens for All News*. Reprinted by permission of the National Gardening Association, 180 Flynn Avenue, Burlington VT 05401 • *University of California Press:* Excerpt from *Saint Francis: Nature Mystic* by Rev. Edward A. Armstrong. Copyright © 1973 by The Regents of the University of California. • *The Estate of Italo Calvino:* Excerpt from *The Baron in the Trees* by Italo Calvino, translated by Archibald Colquhoun. Reprinted by permission of Wylie, Aitken & Stone, Inc. on behalf of the Estate of Italo Calvino.

Library of Congress Cataloging-in-Publication Data

Nabhan, Gary Paul.
Songbirds, truffles, and wolves : an American naturalist in Italy / Gary Paul Nabhan.
p.   cm.
ISBN 0-679-41585-8
1. Tuscany and Umbria (Italy)—Description and travel.   2. Natural history—Italy—Tuscany and Umbria.   3. Nabhan, Gary Paul—Journeys —Italy—Tuscany and Umbria.
I. Title.
DG975.U5N33   1993
914.5'6504929—dc20   92-50783

Book Design by M. Kristen Bearse
Map by John A. Field

Manufactured in the United States of America
First Edition
9 8 7 6 5 4 3 2 1

This book is for Ginger Harmon, who walked with me down the ancient trails trod by Francesco di Bernardone, by bird hunters and truffle grubbers, and by rare wolves

Contents

Acknowledgments

I'd like to express my gratitude to the many Italian residents I met and talked with, particularly the rural people of Tuscany and Umbria, for sharing their knowledge of the land with me. Particular thanks go to Pepé Esquinas-Alcazar and his neighbors in Sacrofano; to Franco La Cecla, Antonio Cacopardo, Gianfranco Bologna, Giannozzo Pucci, John and Beth Romer, Mary Simeti, Giuseppe Barbera, Faith Willinger, Francesco Fiorucci, Emilia Valenti, Luigi Boitani, and Nancy Harmon Jenkins. The staff of World Wildlife Fund/Italy, Assisi Nature Council, Assisi Bird Campaign, the University of Perugia, and the Forestry Programs of Tuscany and Umbria for background information on a variety of topics. The libraries of the Desert Botanical Garden, the Yale School of Forestry and Environmental Studies, and the United Nations Food and Agriculture Organization provided difficult-to-find references.

At home, Jane Cole, Solomon Katz, Sandra Anagnostakis, Nelson Foster, David Wilcove, Roy Gasnick, Paul Shepard, Terry Tempest Williams, Amadeo Rea, Richard Nelson, Sara St. Antoine, and Jack Turner provided information and insight. Kevin Dahl, Jennifer Powers-Murphy, Alison Macondray, and Caroline Wilson helped with the scrambling of final draft submissions; Ross Humphreys and Susan Lowell gave me a hideaway in which to write undisturbed. Fellowships from the MacArthur Foundation and the Pew Memorial Trust bought time. But it was the faith in me by Caroline Wilson, Ginger Harmon, Jack Shoemaker, and Tim Schaffner which pulled me through this one. Jack—it was your idea to get me out of the desert to see what I could find. Look what you've done!

Introduction:
Trekking on Unfamiliar Ground

his, my friends, is a pilgrim's journal, from a journey taken by two Americans across Mediterranean terrain. In September 1990, Ginger Harmon and I walked nearly two hundred miles through the heartland of Italy, the provinces of Tuscany and Umbria; additional time in Italy allowed me to cover side roads alone, interviewing many other country people.

It was not simply a feel for modern Italy

we were after. We were also treading on holy ground, for our route followed the historic Franciscan Way from the mountain hermitages of La Verna, east of Florence, to Assisi, the birthplace of the legendary Francesco di Petro Bernardone. For twenty years, my imagination had wandered those hills as I read story after story about the rovings and ramblings of my favorite saint. I had planned this pilgrimage for two years before we undertook it, and I was fortunate that a veteran saunterer like Ginger Harmon was not only available that September but also amenable to filling her boot heels and fingernails with Mediterranean soil.

Thoreau would have liked Ginger's capacity to saunter and would have agreed that she was ideal company on such a pilgrimage. As he wrote in "Walking": "I have met with but one or two persons in the course of my life who understood the art of Walking, that is, of taking walks,—who had the genius, so to speak, for *sauntering*: which word is beautifully derived 'from idle people who roved about the country, in the Middle Ages, and asked charity, under pretense of going *à la Sainte Terre*,' to the Holy Land, till the children exclaimed, 'There goes a Sainte-Terrer,' a Saunterer, a Holy-Lander."

Ginger had this genius, but for those who knew anything about Ginger or me prior to this joint venture, our point of departure as well as our partnership would have seemed most unlikely. Some would have guessed that we had been blown off course, beginning to backpack where we did, in Florence. Ginger Harmon is better known for leading high-elevation treks through Nepal or for scrambling through the rocks of the San Rafael Swell of Utah than for walking the furrows of Tuscan cornfields and Umbrian orchards. Still, despite her desert and alpine reputation, she had actually spent a month in the forested hills and valleys of northern and central Italy during each of the last four decades. Ginger had backpacked fifteen hundred miles across Europe in 1984, while coauthoring a Sierra Club account of the Grande Randonnée Cinq (GR-5) trail from the North Sea to the Mediterranean.

Ginger first became known to me as one of the elder activists and hands-on enthusiasts of the wilderness conservation movement in the American Southwest, but she soon became a confidante while I was recovering from a divorce. She knew how to help me without intruding, and she knew how to keep me moving whenever the pain began to set in. She was present when I first met the woman whom I have recently wed, but many times between these two marriages, she assured me that I should not try to set a bond too quickly while my heart was still healing. Although small-framed and a number of years my senior, Ginger continues to outwalk me and most other postpuberty males. In addition, Ginger grasped a fair amount of Italian history, and from having helped start the Piatti restaurants in California, knew enough of the country's food and wine legacy to keep us from being starved, poisoned, or foiled by façades on our journey. She also paced us so that all that delicious fare didn't leave us looking as corpulent as a Pavarotti; in fact, the balance she has developed between exploring hiking trails and exploring ethnic foods fit me to a T.

Walking has long been my sport, but southern Europe was as familiar to me as left field; I was clearly in a new ballpark—or perhaps out of my league altogether. Except for a brief stint in Rome working as a seed expert for the United Nations Food and Agriculture Organization the year before, I had for two decades behaved like a dogmatic, dyed-in-the-wool Americanist, sneering at the slightest suggestion that European traditions had contributed anything at all to the quality of my life or to the quality of the lives around me. I had been immersed in Native American landscapes and cultures, learning their foods, their farming, and their fables.

Although my Nabhan kin are of recent Mediterranean derivation—Lebanese refugees from conscription during the Ottoman War—I had seldom given the "Old World" much formal notice or credence. Yet the more time I spent with Native American families and friends, the clearer it became that my respect for their traditions would never be enough to allow me to think, speak, dream, or farm as they do. I was simply not Native American by genes or by upbringing, no matter how "native" I was becoming in my adopted desert home.

As naturalist-author Barry Lopez once wisely instructed me, each of us has the capacity to offer the best from our own culture to others around us. It finally dawned on me that my Native American friends kept in touch with me not simply because I appreciated their cultures and knew something of their land but because they were also curious about the sensibilities that I carried with me from my own background. Of mixed European and Arab descent, I had grown up amid a fun-loving, food-oriented Lebanese clan barely one generation removed from the "old country." My grandfather and several of my uncles had been fruit peddlers for the ethnic communities rimming the Great Lakes; I had not followed directly in their footsteps but had gone off to agricultural college before I became a cross-cultural seed trader.

Growing up where Swedes, eastern European Jews,

southern blacks, and Mexicans had settled along the Pota-
watomi trail, I had spent virtually my entire childhood playing
in cross-cultural contexts. Yet my memories of other families
of Mediterranean origin remain the most vivid. The little girl
who first let me be her "doctor" when we were five was
Greek. An Italian American sailor from Brooklyn rented the
basement of our house when I was young, and when his
equally Italian bride arrived, I would often run my toys across
their floor while they were cooking and arguing. Whenever
my parents left town, a Sicilian neighbor would look after
my brothers and me, barking at us in broken English and
feeding us spicy deep-dish pizzas unlike anything the local
pizza parlors offered at the time. My childhood was filled
with a fragrance and a syntax derived as much from the
Mediterranean as from my Lake Michigan home.

As a child, when I heard relatives and neighbors speak
of the "old country," I imagined a dry, dusty land where
white-haired elders sat in ancient kitchens loaded with filo-
dough pastries, goat cheese, vegetables curing in garlic
and olive oil, freshly butchered lamb, and anise-flavored
liqueurs—an image that sprang from the stories of the
younger immigrant generation who had left behind the old
and infirm. I could never see people my own age in it, only
elders left without anyone younger to share a meal with
them.

Now, as an adult, I began to ask myself if I too had
turned my back on these elders, on the roots of my own
ethnicity. Had I been ignoring the admirable values that my
immigrant kin and neighbors had gleaned from the old country? Undoubtedly, some of those values had become the
cornerstones of my own sensibilities at an early age. Perhaps

those values were still rock solid, if hidden, and perhaps they were more obvious to my Native American friends than they were to me.

As a nomadic naturalist roaming around the desert borderlands between Mexico and the U.S. Southwest, I had become a Westerner in the American sense of the word but had not completely reckoned with the larger West—that of Western civilization. It was a civilization that, for better or worse, had been cradled by Mediterranean peoples and nurtured on Mediterranean foods as much as I had been shaped by the multiethnic neighborhoods of my childhood. And so, I made my way to Italy, in part to ponder my Mediterranean roots, and in part to learn of the land of my saint, San Francisco.

It was in that American West that I first became familiar with Saint Francis. Coming off my first wilderness experience in the early seventies—at a time when *zazen* (sitting meditation) was the only religious pursuit I would stand for—I had happened on this quotation from the Umbrian saint in a pile of paper in a Utah gas station: "All which you used to avoid will bring you great sweetness and exceeding joy." I was suddenly struck by this notion that each of us needs to make peace with the peoples, the creatures, and the conditions of this world that we are inclined to loathe, fear, or flee. Happening on this Franciscan riddle was enough to spark my studies of the life of Saint Francis. Here was a historic figure who could do more for me than adorn my birdbath; he might inspire me to live more fully engaged with all parts of this world. I began to seek out everything I could read about Saint Francis, from the stories of Kazantzakis to the historiographies of the famous former mayor of Assisi, Fortini.

A couple of years later, while a guest teacher at an Indian boarding school on the Tohono O'odham reservation, I reluctantly stopped in at a nearby Franciscan mission to pass on to a priest a message from a mutual friend. I thought that *I* hated the idea of missionaries, but I found that this priest hated it even more. His goals were to be among indigenous people for only a short while, to assure them that their spirituality could be expressed in any combination of native and Western terms and symbols with which they felt comfortable, and then to make the presence there of "outside missionaries" obsolete forevermore. This gentle heretic was soon asked to leave the reservation by a bishop who thought he was "subversive," but he has continued training lay communities to take responsibility for their own spirituality wherever he has lived since then. I ended up visiting this priest frequently, and I gradually became friends with the O'odham families in the community he assisted.

I soon learned that most O'odham Indians were Catholics of the Franciscan persuasion, not because they had first been missionized by Franciscans—the Jesuits can claim that honor—but because Franciscans had planted the seeds of captivating stories that had taken root in their spirituality. Following the 1767 Jesuit expulsion from the Americas, Franciscans like Padre Garces had arrived in the desert and adopted the O'odham forms of food, shelter, and travel as their own, seeking less to convert the Native Americans than to add another element to their lives. Over the next two centuries, as missionary presence declined, a "San Francisco" cult or folk tradition emerged in northern Mexico and southern Arizona, based on wooden statues of the Jesuit San Xavier but with the dress and the traits of San Francisco de Assis. Even today, my elderly O'odham neighbors tell of a simply dressed, barefoot saint who wandered through the desert, speaking to animals, helping victimized maidens, and serving the poor.

The O'odham themselves wander through the desert each October to pay their respect to a shrine for Saint Francis in Magdalena, Sonora, Mexico. I have celebrated the Feast of Saint Francis in Magdalena several times with O'odham and Yaqui Indian friends and have walked parts of the pilgrimage route on three different occasions. Here I found a blend of New World and Old World traditions that comforted my soul: a stroll through the desert and its traditional farm country at the end of the rainy season, when fruits are ripening and seedheads are drying in the sun; a pilgrimage to offer thanks for rains abundant enough to guarantee a harvest for humans, other mammals, and birds alike; a cool, all-night celebration with music, dance, and prayer at the end of a season of sweat, dust, and heat in the desert fields.

There was something universal about the ways in which that Sonoran folk pilgrimage and festival met the spiritual needs of O'odham, Yaqui, Hispanic, and even Anglo residents of the desert country. As Yi-fu Tuan has written, "Close-knit social life offers many rewards, but it also imposes severe constraints. . . . People [from traditional villages] seek liberation from the common routines of life. In premodern times, they can do so through two practices: one is the festival, and the other is the pilgrimage. In a festival, people move from the ordinary world of work and social obligations to another of communion with sky and earth and with nature's gods. In pilgrimage, they abandon the local community to undertake a demanding and dangerous journey for a 'center out there,' a sacred center and a strange place at which pilgrims, all strangers to each other, nevertheless feel a common bond; they have moved from a local community to something larger and freer—to *communitas*."

The need for *communitas* is not restricted to premodern peasants; such pilgrimages and festivals continue to be vital in nearly all countries of the world. As I walked along the traditional pilgrimage route in the Mexican desert, I often wondered whether there were similar peregrinations going on halfway around the world near Assisi on behalf of the same saint. Or was he the same saint, after all? Was the odd mix of Franciscan and Jesuit dressing on Native American folklore anything like the saint that Italians claimed for their own? Although rooted in Italian soil, the legend of that peculiarly European saint had been embellished with early Irish and French "nature-saint" stories consistent with his own character. Idly, I dreamed of finding a parallel pilgrimage route through Umbria so that I could someday compare the traditions that Saint Francis had engendered on both sides of the Atlantic.

During my estrangement from my first wife in 1988 and 1989, I spent nearly a year and a half going through an initiation course to become a secular Franciscan "tertiary." Feeling as though I had lost my family and home, I sought some way of healing and of learning how to deal freshly with the world; it was then that I was drawn deeper into Franciscanism, with its voluntary vows of poverty, conscientious objection to violence, and humility in the presence of other creatures. Third-order Franciscan lay brothers do not retreat to the cloister, take vows of celibacy, or necessarily give up their former professions; rather, they remain in the "marketplace" and seek to enrich ordinary life through the inspiration of Saint Francis, the *poverello*, or "little poor one."

Like others in my class of novices, I was instructed to devote time to helping others who were neglected or abused. Yet my wish to work with the poorest of the poor—endangered plants that had not yet received any legal protection—was hardly met with effusive acceptance from those who were initiating me. I sensed that many current members of the order treated it as just another Catholic social service organization, like the Knights of Columbus or Saint Vincent de Paul. The premise that followers of Saint Francis might honor his legacy by helping species other than human beings seemed to them quaint and peripheral, at best. Disappointed by their reaction and still uneasy about participating in any institutionalized aspect of the Catholic faith itself, I decided to postpone my formal request to join the order until I could visit the birthplace of Saint Francis. I hoped that there I would be able to resolve my ambivalence.

Thus, I prepared to walk through the Tuscan and Umbrian mountains in order to deal with my own wounds as much as to see their wonders. And in planning the journey, I began to realize that the Italian land itself was a land of ancient wounds. Environmental historian Carolyn Merchant has argued that the Mediterranean basin is where the desecration and "death" of nature occurred in Western thought: dominionistic lords deflowered and deforested the wildlands of southern Europe, just as monotheistic missionaries converted the animists. So, I thought, why not mourn the death of my first marriage in a place where the scarred body of nature first fell? Perhaps a full-fledged wake would enable me to chart a new course for myself and to envision a fresh relation with other beings.

At the least, the pilgrimage would allow me to confront a track that may be as old as our species. In *The Songlines*, Bruce Chatwin suggested that "Natural Selection has designed us—from the structure of our brain cells to the structure of our big toe—for a career of seasonal journeys *on foot* through a blistering land."

While Mediterranean landscapes may not have been blistering lands when such pilgrimage traditions began, they have since been blistered by innumerable abuses. Some historians claim that the Western tendency to control or kill wild nature has now been made manifest on every continent, but it is most evident in the Mediterranean region. As final as this "death of nature" pronouncement seems, I would wager that wildness remains a hard beast to kill, especially if a few tenacious supporters have been hiding in the woodwork all along. However many times all of Europe has been condemned by the categorical statements of American environmental historians, I was holding out for the possibility that the folk science of Umbrian peasants still contained considerable earthbound wisdom. In selecting our pilgrimage route, we aimed for areas where such wisdom might be manifest. The test would be to see if that ethereal wisdom had been translated into tangible signs within their habitats. I wanted to know if the folk knowledge of nature—and the example of Saint Francis—that had accumulated over generations had served Italian farmers, foragers, and foresters well enough to have kept their land from losing all of its wildness.

This notion had already been considered and promptly

dismissed by environmental philosopher René Dubos. In his eyes, "the teachings of Saint Francis had little if any influence on the destruction of wildlife by Italians and other Europeans." Curiously, other informed observers were not so sure that nothing tangible had lasted from the little revolution that Francesco di Bernardone had begun around the year 1205.

The Franciscan tradition was taken seriously by at least one biological historian, Alfred Crosby, who coined a now-famous term, *the Columbian exchange*, to refer to the swap of plants, animals, and diseases between the Americas and Eurasia. During my first personal encounter with Dr. Crosby, our conversation had quickly turned to this interest, which we had both come upon independently. Crosby's solemnity and sincerity spoke out above the chatter at the cocktail party being thrown in our honor by a mutual friend in Austin, Texas.

"After years of documenting and interpreting the ecological imperialism that Europe has imposed on the rest of the world, I recently had to take a break from all that and ask myself a different question." I remember him sighing, then framing his question in this way: "Isn't there any historic figure or folk tradition you can find in Europe that has been a counterforce to this tendency to devastate the world?"

"Did you find one?" I asked.

"When I began to read about Saint Francis of Assisi, I think I did," he said.

If Saint Francis was indeed a counterforce against ecological imperialism—as his title as patron saint of ecology may imply—then he should have inspired his followers to a greater sensitivity toward the land and its creatures. For me, the success of the Franciscan tradition could not be judged solely on the basis of Francesco di Bernardone's words taken out of their context and left dangling like abstractions. I wanted to see how his followers saw those words expressed in the flesh of the land, its soils, its fruits, its wild birds, and other wild creatures. Would central Italy show any signs that the earthward tendencies of Saint Francis had actually been put into practice?

I realized that the land there would not now feel, smell, or look as it had when Francesco di Bernardone had known it. The Strada Francescana, or Franciscan Way, once a rude footpath, was now for the most part paved. Not far from Assisi, a dam was being built that would block one of the longest unpaved stretches from Gubbio. However, few pilgrims today walk more than the last twenty miles of this historic trail, and they do that segment only once a year, just before the Feast of Saint Francis in October.

I would begin the pilgrimage with a train ride from Genoa but would not begin to walk until after Ginger had caught up with me in Florence. While on my own in Florence, I learned that this was where modern forms of public accounting, taxation, and administration of social services had taken their present shape. I soon realized that I had come to do another kind of accounting, an independent audit of the gains and losses the land had suffered over the last five to seven centuries. While I would use neither numbers nor dollars to express these gains and losses, I could read of the landscape's richness and bankruptcies by other means.

It would take me considerably longer to be able to speak and read adequately the Italian dialects and their nuances, but I was ecologically literate enough to read the Italian landscape itself. Twenty years of plant exploration, mixed with bouts of ecological and ethnographic research, trekking, and tending gardens, had given me the rudimentary skills for reading the Tuscan and Umbrian scripts imprinted on the land. Ginger's earlier walks across Europe had given her complementary skills in reading the terrain and the vigor of human communities along our route.

Of course, the country people of Italy—the *contadini*— have a landscape literacy all their own. They can detect where truffles might be hiding by reading the microtopography beneath oak trees. Some farmers are able to gauge how much moisture is stored in the mass of a hill by observing which trees are doing poorly and are showing temporary signs of wilt. The same forested hill, to Ginger and me, might only be read as evidence of secondary forest regeneration, as weedy trees that have colonized a field abandoned after World War II. We could not possibly have the maps that local peasants carry in their heads, nor could we have an inkling of the floral and faunal changes occurring from season to season, year to year, or decade to decade.

The tension between the local ecological literacy of Italian peasants and our own, between the Old World and the New, would set up some revealing polarities. We had no way of knowing local land-use history as well as they did, but we could see its results, sometimes, when they could not. What we lacked in mental maps, we hoped to make up for by guiding ourselves between the cultural poles of this compass. We would know how well the compass worked when we arrived at our destination—healed or further scarred.

Songbirds, Truffles, and Wolves

Chapter 1

*The saunterer, in the good sense, is no more vagrant than the
meandering river, which is all the while sedulously seeking the
shortest course to the sea.*

HENRY DAVID THOREAU

Beyond Columbus:
American Tracks
on Mediterranean Soils

 t was Columbus Day, and I was adrift in a place where I knew no one and for which I had no map. I stumbled down foreign streets, disoriented by the low clouds, until I smelled where the breeze was coming from and saw where the Mediterranean gulls were circling.

I had wanted to reach the shoreline or at least arrive at some landmark that would appease the sense of loss in my heart. I *was* lost and *had* lost; this feeling had come with my recent divorce and its aftermath of homelessness. But now I could only trudge along, a vagrant with too much baggage, a street Arab wearing too many clothes. The heat and humidity were getting the best of me, although I tried to convince myself that I was hot on the trail of something momentous. I straggled past the statue of the Primal Navigator and past a dozen Columbus Day posters plastered to the walls, wrinkled like the wet shirt beneath my sportscoat. I paused a moment in front of the Trattoria dei Pescatori, the fragrances of calamari, garlic, shrimp, fish, and olive oil wafting into the street and assaulting my taste buds. For the first time in hours, I paid attention to my hunger.

I put down my luggage for a moment and breathed in the smells of the harbor, the sea, and its foods. I had come here to be refreshed, but as I closed my eyes, I felt a continuous pooling of sweat on my brow and a tiredness that reached into my bones. When I opened my eyes again and looked around, I was confronted with a giant billboard. Its headline read, "Vagabond Jeans: The World in Your Pocket," over a map of where I had been living in the American desert. I had come halfway around the world to find myself in Genoa, exorcising the ghost of Columbus, a man who had invaded my homeland and disrupted the lives of my native neighbors. Yet when I arrived at *his* birthplace, it was an apparition of my own country that stared me in the face. I began to contemplate how thoughts of this Columbus make our views of the world loop back upon themselves.

"Vagabond Jeans." I pondered the vagabond nature of the man celebrated by the Columbus Day posters, a hero now claimed by Genoa and a dozen other towns as a native son. He was a man who, throughout most of his adulthood, had no permanent home other than the sea, who scarcely kept contact with his *terra mater*, and who hardly used his *lingua mater* after his departure from this port.

Wincing, I realized that vagabonds, wayfarers, explorers, and conquerors have become heroes around the world, while those who stay put—Italian farmers and authentic American cowhands who require such work jeans—are ignored, distorted, or derided. I winced because for all my professed allegiance to place, I too had become a vagabond. Scanning the ad's map, I spotted the names of towns where I have worked and lived. But here those names had been reduced to exotica, having no more meaning for the locals than "Genoa" had had for me when I struck out for this place.

I stepped past the giant map. Suddenly, the billboards, restaurant façades, and cityscapes receded into the background. I had arrived at what I wanted to see, to smell, to absorb: the Mediterranean of the Ligurian coast, the seascape that had compelled Cristoforo Colombo to leave his nearby home more than five hundred years ago.

I remembered the words of Native American poet Joy Harjo, who, when visiting the Italian coast, wrote, "It could all be some version of a word for goodbye. Genoa staggered north of there. Did Columbus say goodbye as he set off to test the limits of the edge of the world? What did he expect to find? The sea at night was a woman who had encountered the nightmare."

Salt stung my nostrils as the waves splashed and sprayed up over the breakwater's riprap. A few colonizing waifs hung onto the rocks: a sea blite, a purslane, a nightshade. Mediterranean gulls circled and dove, fluttered and circled again above the closest strand of seaweed bobbing in the intertidal shallows.

Beyond the gulls, beyond the breakers, turquoise water stretched clear to the southern horizon. The sun's image shimmered, distorted by the surging surface of the sea. The rhythm of the waves hypnotized me as nothing on land could do.

I reflected on how that same ceaseless rhythm must have captivated Columbus the boy, one of many who became converted to seafaring ways while growing up in Genoa. *Dopo la Burrasca* (After the Storm), a nineteenth-century oil painting by the Genoan artist Luigi Bechi, captures the excitement of three local youths exploring the Ligurian shoreline. One lad proudly displays his gleanings from the flotsam and jetsam that have been beached by a torrent. A young maiden between the two boys pauses, transfixed, perhaps because she has just culled from the murky water the dazzling necklace in her hands. But the image is ambivalent. It is just as plausible that she is ready to plunge it underwater, letting the waves release it to another world.

I wondered how Columbus dealt with such feelings as a child—the sense of living on the edge, of trying to arrive at the right place at the right time for "discovery's sake." Was it possible to grow up on such a coast without ever longing to drift out into another, far larger world? While growing up on the Lake Michigan shore, I had often sat transfixed, staring at the undulating horizon, wondering what lay beyond the open water. The Mediterranean surely must mesmerize many of its youth, who then go off seeking what lies beyond, just as Columbus did.

Of course, I was not the first to wonder about the sea's

intoxicating effect on Columbus. Joy Harjo caught this drunkenness: "I could see Columbus and his teetering ship setting off with such bravado, the same bravado that created the leaning tower, that beat the child into womanhood." This bravado is not found in Columbus alone but in anyone having the imperialistic urge to conquer and alter a foreign land and its native people. All of us have been left awash in the turbulent wake of the conquistadors. We are like those children after the storm, having to sort riches from the rubbish, unaware of the dimensions of some shipwreck nearby. When all is told, Columbus will be seen as just one of many paradoxical players involved in that tragic shipwreck of conquerors and the conquered.

I returned from my reverie, feeling the weight of my own baggage. I had come here as a pilgrim, to mourn my own visceral history as much as to learn more of it. But for the moment, I had to find a place to pitch my luggage so that I could wander less encumbered through the port.

Later in the day, I visited a simple stone house, this Colombo's reputed place of birth. The entire neighborhood was being renovated in order to absorb the interest that the five-hundredth anniversary of Columbus's sailing would bring to Liguria, a land long considered a separate country but now nominally a part of Italy. Fortunately, I had arrived too early to be swept into the celebratory whirlpool. For the time being, the vicinity of *casa di Colombo* was about as pretty as a bleached blonde in curlers: scaffolding was up everywhere, and piles of lumber, stone, piping, and paint had been assembled to doll up the neighborhood.

Nevertheless, the pictorial quality of the reputed birth-place would leave something to be desired regardless of how much money were poured into it. The house was surrounded by a parking lot full of Pandas, Fiats, and motorbikes; buildings plastered with posters bearing Marxist propaganda; and a branch office of a mercantile bank—all in all, a cluttered and lackluster scene. Distracted, I ventured down the narrow alleys between the Colombo home and the seafront, following a maze of four- and six-story apartments that had been refurbished, repaired, or patched together far too many times. Laundry was strung between the flats as if clotheslines held the whole neighborhood together. The pedestrian passage-ways below these dripping clothes were too narrow for even the most minuscule of European cars to navigate safely.

Around the corner from the cradle of Columbus, I fol-lowed two nuns down a winding lane and into an open-air fruit market. Asking for pity if not for business, two of the vendors explained how they park themselves in the middle of the small plaza every Saturday from dawn to dusk, re-gardless of how much they sell. When the nuns offered them no sympathy, they turned to me, hawking their wares. They were as anxious for their story to be heard as they were to make a sale.

It was among these people that I found evidence of the legacy of the Columbian exchange that I had not sensed on the timeless seafront or garnered from the carved stone plaque embedded in the wall of the Colombo home. That legacy may be touched on in some history books, but here it was palpable: foods from various foreign lands jumbled together in one market stall as if they had all come from the same patch of Eden: cucumbers, squashes, avocados, apples, morel mushrooms, and pomegranates.

While the merchants chattered and gestured at me, my mind drifted into an exercise that I had often practiced in my recently suspended career as a seed vendor, back in the time when I was married, with a home and a large garden of glorious vegetables. I would occasionally leave these touchstones to go off on botanical adventures, recruiting more fruits for trials at home or at a local experimental farm. I had made my living as a plant explorer of sorts—that is, as a seed and fruit collector for various gene banks around the world—so it was my calling to survey the diversity in fruit and vegetable markets and to learn where various crops had originated. I had no professional aspirations to collect the seeds or tubers present in this market, but my eyes involuntarily inventoried the vegetable stalls; once trained, perhaps they could see the world no other way. I worked over the shapes and mapped the origins of every drupe, pome, stalk, tuber, bloom, and sprout.

"Pomegranates, once rooted only in the Arabian peninsula." The monologue in my head ticked them off. "Cucumbers, cradled in India. Pears, nurtured in Asia Minor. Tomatoes, from the western watersheds of South America, diversified in Mexico. Avocados, dropping out of Central American trees"—and the stallkeeper caught me pinching them for ripeness.

"You like my avocados? I get them flown in. Freshly picked. Delicious . . ." Of the many kinds of produce exhibited on his tables, most were migrants from foreign lands. I began to feel less like the only odd duck present.

Then one particular fruit caught my eye and brought tears to it. The sight of a bowlful of "Indian fig" prickly pear fruit instantly made me homesick for the borderlands between the United States and Mexico that had been my romping grounds for two decades. In those desert lands, native prickly pears, both wild and cultivated, are as characteristic of the landscape as Italian cypress and rosemary were here.

"How much will it be for just one *ficodindia?*" I asked the old woman tending the stand. She stared at me for a moment, puzzled, so I added an explanation, "It reminds me of my homeland in the desert."

"Sicily?" the woman inquired. "You don't talk like any Sicilian. And you look like an American tourist."

"Grazie!" I replied, making a mock bow. I realized that my camera bag, poorly tailored sportscoat, and baggy blue jeans broadcast my foreign identity. "No, I'm no Sicilian. I live on the border between the United States of America and the Republic of Mexico." I offered this in cracked Italian, which rolled into Tex-Mex Spanish when I reached the "República Mexicana." "These fruit, they originally come from the deserts there."

"Well, then," she said, eyeing me, "I'll give you one of them for 150 lire. You buy the bowlful, I'll give you all of them for 500 lire."

"No room in my pockets," I shrugged, pantomiming that they were already stuffed. At the same time, I imagined the thorny problem of tucking prickly pears into my pockets. "Here, 150 lire."

I pulled out my pocketknife and began to peel the fruit in a spiral, the way a Mexican friend had taught me. A finger on top, a finger below, and I could avoid a mess of tiny hairlike stickers stabbing my flesh.

"No, no! That's not how you do it! Give it to me! You'll butcher it like that!" A rather well-dressed man who had been standing nearby suddenly intervened on behalf of the prickly pear. He must have caught the tail end of my conversation with the fruit vendor, for he began to lecture me in a mix of broken English and some dialect other than the local Ligurian. He gestured for the fruit and for my pocketknife. Before I knew it, he had lopped off both ends of the fruit, cut it in half lengthwise, peeled off the prickly skins on each half, and tossed the peelings on the pavement. He plopped the two clean, juicy halves of the fruit into my palm.

"Did I hear you say these fruit are from *your* homeland? What do you mean? I'm a professional geographer, I know where they're from. We call them Indian fig, so perhaps that's why you think that they're from the West Indies, from American Indians, you know? Well, that's not so. I'm from Sicily, I know. You must understand that the climate of Sicily is very special, and for a long time, Sicily was in geographic isolation. For these reasons, many special plants developed there—what do you say, *evolved?*—that could not have originated anywhere else. Sure, you see them in other countries now, Morocco, even Greece, perhaps they have been taken to where you live, too. But I'm telling you, this *ficodindia*, it's special, it's a Sicilian original!"

The loquacious professor was not alone in his opinion that prickly pears were an ancient Sicilian crop. As recently as 1988, Italian historians have argued that certain obscure fruits noted by Pliny and Theophrastus could only have been

Sicilian prickly pears. However, other Sicilian scholars have conceded that there is no good evidence of this plant on their island prior to a seventeenth-century still life, painted well after the Columbian exchange of crops between continents. Yet the progeny of prickly pears introduced to greater Europe between 1492 and 1568 are now easy to distinguish from their American progenitors. Most have twice the juicy pulp per volume of seed mass that do the majority of prickly pears from the American deserts, wild or cultivated. The fruits are considered a delicacy, and for a while last century, they were selected for alcohol production by Sicilian winemakers. The flowers have been used as a diuretic in the Sicilian countryside, and the pads are still used by peasants to treat whooping cough. For over three centuries, Sicilian prickly pears have undergone cultural selection for these uses and have adapted to a Mediterranean climate.

Curiously, other uses of prickly pears, from the ancient traditions of American Indians, never arrived from the southern United States and Mexico. For instance, Sicilians do not cut up the pads to make tender vegetable *nopalitos*, nor do they glean the red cochineal dye from insect-infested cactus plants. From the cliff faces above Palermo to the patio gardens in the valleys, *ficodindia* varieties have taken on lives of their own, apart from those originally found in Mexico or the U.S. Southwest.

So this Sicilian geographer, my ethnocentric antagonist and instant friend, knew what was peculiar to his homeland and considered it indigenous to his culture. He assumed that the prickly pears now found along the Mediterranean coasts, like the swordlike century plants, were not the same as those of the American continents or West Indies.

In a sense, they *are* as native to Sicily as Sioux Indian warriors on horseback are to the Great Plains, as native as Navajo sheepherders and rug weavers are to the Colorado plateau. One's sense of nativity is not a cut-and-dried matter, based only on historic fact. What is or what is not part of a particular cultural heritage is determined as much by mouth and heart as it is by text and brain. As children, we begin to pick up clues as to what our kinfolk hold familiar and dear, as opposed to what they consider foreign, alien, or peregrine. We sharpen these definitions as we enter into adulthood and carry them with us wherever we go.

After more than a decade of visiting and living in Tuscany, food historian Nancy Harmon Jenkins spoke to me about her sense of the antiquity of foods now considered characteristic of Tuscan cuisine: "It is hard now to imagine what the Tuscan diet was like before contact with the New World, since so many mainstays were introduced after Columbus." Indeed, many of the ingredients originating in the Americas are now so steeped in Tuscan traditions that the country folk themselves cannot conceive of a time when their forefathers lacked tomatoes, green beans, and peppers on their tables, next to the bread, wine, cheese, and olive oil.

Later, as I traveled on from Liguria to Tuscany on my way to meet Ginger, I came into landscapes tinted with shades of America. These central Italian provinces, considered some of the most colorful rural regions in all of Europe, have incorporated numerous elements of the New World and shaped them as their own.

Taking a slow-moving train, I tried deciphering the global biogeography encoded in the colors of the Tuscan landscape's mosaic. I had just awakened from a nap, and my eyes had barely adjusted to the brilliant light pouring through the windows. So at first, the contents of the fields alongside the tracks were blurred, a Cézanne mosaic of sienna, hot green, and chocolate brown. As details came into focus, I realized that the splashes of yellow staining the wetter depressions were the same weedy sunflowers that had followed Mormon wagon trains across the Great Plains, clear to the Beulah Land of central Utah. The rusts of drying stalks belonged to *granoturco*—Indian corn—with midwestern carelessweed cropping up in its midst. The gray, cone-shaped trees on the horizon, punctuated in a windbreak with the exclamation marks of Italian cypress, were none other than Arizona cypress transplants that had traveled an eastward trajectory set in motion by the response of the U.S. Soil Conservation Service to the Dust Bowl in the thirties.

When I turned my attention from fields to garden plots, I saw them crowded with tepee-like tripods of trellised vegetables. These were dappled with the greens and reds of plum tomatoes and cranberry beans, descendants of seeds brought from Latin America to European botanical gardens four centuries ago. Once the curiosities of feudal lords and their hired naturalists, these indigenes of the Neotropics were now found in nearly every northern Italian garden, from the highest hillside farm to the darkest innards of factory towns in the valleys.

All these observations were not to deny the tenacious presence of olive orchards, vineyards, and artichoke crowns, which abound now just as they did in the centuries before Columbus transported the first American crop seeds back to the Spanish queen. Columbus could never have guessed that it would be the vegetal wealth, not the minerals, of the lands he had encountered that would transform European places as nothing else had done. Not since the arrival of Christianity—or perhaps, since the diffusion of agriculture from the Middle East five thousand years earlier—had Europe undergone material changes of the magnitude brought about by those seeds.

To his death, Columbus himself remained ignorant of the plants that would soon become so valuable to the peoples of the Mediterranean. He admitted that his failure to be able to tell different plants apart from one another "gives me the greatest grief in the world, for I see a thousand sorts of trees . . . and . . . recognize only . . . aloes." His aloes, unfortunately, were not true aloes; instead, they were the visually similar but unrelated century plants native only to the New World. Now, however, these plants form hedges along pathways up to Greek temples in Sicily, and decorate Christian monasteries in northern Italy. Century plants and prickly pears have naturalized along the Italian coastlines, no doubt becoming as troublesome in places as Mediterranean weeds have become in California and the Arizona deserts. My career as a plant explorer had made me painfully aware of such waifs, orphans, transplants, and immigrants, which tend to inhabit the most scarred and depleted habitats where stable "old growth" species can no longer survive.

Aldo Leopold once wrote about how ecologists often suffer from an acute consciousness of landscape disruptions, an affliction quite similar to a crippling self-consciousness: "One of the penalties of an ecological education is that one lives alone in a world of wounds. Much of the damage inflicted on land is quite invisible to laymen. An ecologist must either harden his shell and make believe that the consequences of science are none of his business, or he must be the doctor who sees the marks of death in a community that believes itself well and does not want to be told otherwise."

I am not one who does well at hardening my shell. Instead, the landscape through which I traveled became the allegory through which I saw my own story being told: the damaged home ground, the uprooted tree of life, the frightened creatures taking flight, the emptied nests, the mournful songs of exiles.

Thus, as I looked around at all the dislocated plants, it seemed to me that the scars on Italian lands had become infested with the weeds sent flying from other disrupted places. Columbus started this biological rummage sale, now so pervasive that few landscapes on earth are entirely free of weeds or vermin from other continents. On the other hand, few kitchen tables maintain a cuisine so pure that they do not include spices and staples from distant lands. The tastes, tints, and fragrances of American floral origin are as deeply implanted in the Mediterranean mentality as they are in the landscape.

Of course, it is not always easy to follow the tracks taken by Neotropical seeds, roots, bulbs, and corms that were trafficked back to European gardens and kitchens. Only a few of the physician-naturalists who studied these plants—Martyr, Oviedo, and Martínez among them—gave us detailed descriptions of the early horticultural and culinary immigrants. Some of the uprooted plants were harbored in European botanical gardens, where their progeny were sooner or later described in herbal compendia or painted for posterity. Still, even the herbals concentrated only on the plants that received the formal attention of nobility due to their pharmacological notoriety, their beauty, or their culinary quality.

It has always been the accepted view of historians that these floral marvels were released to the masses only after the royalty had fussed enough over them. But my own experience has been that most plant introductions happen by more informal means. Lorraine Lilja has envisioned the Ellis Island scene from the early twentieth century, in which European emigrants smuggled into America their most precious heirloom garden crops:

> They sat patiently waiting on the hard wood benches of Ellis Island. Their faces reflected the nervousness they felt, but their eyes were shining with hope. Maria de Salla stood near a window, her arms stiffly pushing fists into the stretched pockets of her black coat. Within one of those clenched palms was the only bit of Italy she could take along: the seeds of a plum tomato that would guarantee decades of manicotti, lasagna, spaghetti marinara, and braciola.
>
> Katie Murphy sat in the front row, her arms encircling a blue-eyed toddler. At the bottom of her canvas sack on the floor were four seed potatoes, the same species that had survived the potato famine, traced back as far as family lore and human memory stretched. There were cabbage seeds in the lining of Karl Schmidt's suitcase, chile peppers in the band of José Sanchez's hat, and rye grains filled the toe of Ivan Ivanovich's wool sock. These brandnew Americans brought along these grains of life that gave them the confidence to start life anew in a strange land.

I remember another encounter with a Sicilian over prickly pears, this time on my home turf. The local newspaper had featured a modest project regarding prickly pear genetic resources that I had initiated at the Desert Botanical Garden. On a hot summer day, as I rested in the dark of my office after several hours of work in the sun, a phone call was directed to me.

"Hello. My name is Pete, Pete Cipriano. I live in Sun City now for fifteen years, but I'm from Palermo. Sicily. You know? Are you the boy that's growing the desert prickly pear to eat the fruit?"

"Yes. Yes, I am . . ."

"Well, you got the wrong one."

"I got the wrong one? Wrong what?"

"Wrong kind. When I came here, I tried a lot of the ones out in the desert, some here around town, too. They're no good to eat, I'm telling you. I'll give you the right one."

"The right one?"

"Sure, the real *ficodindia*, it's from Sicily. I grew it from seed. Big juicy fruit, you'll see. Come on over and prune my plants—they're twelve feet tall and getting too big for me—and I'll give you some of those pads to plant. To start mine, I didn't have pads because the customs took the ones I tried to bring back from Palermo one time."

"How did you get the seed past the customs, then?"

"I didn't."

"You didn't?"

"My uncle did it for me. He was bishop in Palermo, a big shot in the Catholic church, you know? They never check the priests, I guess. He brought me seeds from three different varieties that he hid in his vestments."

"I see . . ."

"You come out to Sun City, and I'll show you how well they grow. Absolutely delicious fruit. The plants are just five years old, and they're taller than my roof. You bring your pruning shears when you come, okay?"

Padres Chini, Salvaterra, Garrucho. Governor Crespo. Viceroy Bucareli. Whether Sicilian, Sardinian, Tridentine, or Ligurian, there were many Mediterranean-born clerics and entrepreneurs who arrived in the Americas at early dates and held some kind of tenure there through the sixteenth, seventeenth, or eighteenth centuries. I cannot imagine that their packages to and from their families did not contain more than words. The dried foods, seeds, and herbal remedies sent to them from Europe were mementos beseeching them to remember their families, their culture, and their upbringing. The seeds and fruit sent back home were talismans meant to bring the foreign into the domain of the familiar. The priest stationed in Mexico who sent his mother a string of dried chiles to hang in her kitchen could then imagine part of his strange new world enveloped and domesticated within his mother's domain. They were love charms and cultural touchstones as much as they were seeds for planting and eating. Thus, they took routes that most of the authorities never learned about.

There were undoubtedly other seeds that did come in official shipments or as ballast filling the bowels of some Spanish galleon. But their stories do not interest me as much as those woven into the warp and woof of family folklore: the oral histories of journeys taken by seeds, foods, and farming traditions, some of them now lost from one place but still sprouting in another.

As I became familiar with Italy, it dawned on me that I might be able to trace the Native American threads that had been stitched into European tapestries—specifically, into the Tuscan and Umbrian countrysides of central Italy. In fact, I realized, I had come here in search of just such lost threads: those that bind the old and the new worlds together.

When I saw them in the fruit stand, I realized that prickly pear fruit linked my desert homeland with the place where I found myself at present. So I bought a few more of them and went off to one side of the plaza to slice and eat them. As I used my knife to cut the juicy flesh out of them, just as my Sicilian professor had instructed, their juices drenched and stained my hands, sweetened and moistened my parched mouth. I finished this modest meal—Mesoamerican in origin but Mediterranean in trajectory—then laced my way back from the Columbus neighborhood to the shipyards and the railroad lines. As the sun set on Columbus Day, I waited for a train bound for Rome, where I would exchange handbags and sportscoat for backpack and field gear. After a brief visit with friends in Rome, I would take another train to Florence, to meet Ginger and begin our sauntering as a pair.

For the moment, however, I was still alone, feeling more like an island unto myself than like one who had arrived on a crowded continent. As the train pulled into the station, I clenched the grips on my suitcases and looked around me: local families were hugging their departing loved ones, bidding them farewell with passionate Italian idioms and gestures.

My stomach tightened with the feeling of being an outsider, exiled from such human bonds.

I took one long step up onto the train, and seeing that the first car was full, I crossed the bridge into the next, where I would stay until I reached Rome.

Interlude 1
Leaving Genoa Behind

We stand together at a place where the failed European system of belief has led us, at the threshold to the endangered world, at limits stretched to breaking. Too much is moving over the edge, species and lives falling over the end of the earth. . . . We have no choice but to face ourselves, history, our fears, and the challenge of change.

LINDA HOGAN

 stood against my bags in the aisles for the first forty-five minutes of the train ride out of Genoa and down the coast to Rome. The passenger cars were all packed, and the voices I heard around me were speaking Italian, German, French, and Spanish. Because Genoa sits on the railroad line between southern France and Rome, travelers from many European countries pass through it. Many of them eventually make

their way to the Vatican for blessings and to Rome's boutiques for shopping. I suddenly felt like I was fully *encountering Europe*, not simply lodged on the Italian peninsula.

I eventually found a vacant seat and pitched my bags atop the luggage rack. I fussed with a prepacked meal of cheese and bread, a salad of lettuce, tomato, and peperoncini chiles, and a bottle of Peroni beer. Opening my journal and recovering a few scraps of paper from my pockets, I transcribed quotations from Italo Calvino on the forest as community, from D. H. Lawrence on the beauty of Tuscan wildflowers, and from Vasco Pratolini on his family's eviction from an apartment in Florence. As night fell, tiredness set in, and I closed my eyes. Yet I could not sleep, for my mind was filled with images of the day, as well as with others from twenty years of foreign travel, and even with voices all around me, I still felt alone, homeless, and interminably "on the road."

I remembered the reason for my digression to visit the birthplace of Columbus: I had wanted to learn of the links that Columbus had with the Franciscan tradition. It has been suggested that Columbus may have been a Franciscan tertiary or at least a novice in the third order, as I myself had labored to become over the past couple of years. In any case, during his time in Portugal, he was strongly influenced by the Order of the Friars Minor—both by their spirituality and by their knowledge of astronomy. In the years prior to his departure for parts unknown in 1492, he and his son Diego spent considerable time at the hilltop monastery of La Rábida. The Franciscans there helped him gain his last hearing with Queen Isabella—the one that finally set his first voyage in motion. On his second voyage, he carried with him the guardian of

La Rábida, as well as other Franciscans, who would begin converting the inhabitants of the West Indies from their native beliefs. A Franciscan was later selected as the first bishop in the Americas and was charged with dispersing missionaries to the various colonies being planned among newfound tribes.

In 1502, well after the conversion of Native Americans and their landscapes had begun, Columbus wrote to Pope Alexander VI to mention that he had personally visited the Garden of Eden on one of his voyages to the New World. Always a more mystic than a rationalist, Columbus had apparently become infected with the apocalyptic fervor of radical Franciscan reformers, who believed that Christianity had become so corrupt in Europe that it could only survive in unspoiled lands elsewhere. They not only wanted the Franciscan orders to return to the earlier, more austere Rule of Saint Francis approved by Pope Honorius III in 1223 but they also wanted to overhaul the entire church. Hoping to muster the support of these reformers, Columbus claimed that he had been given a divine calling to rediscover the garden and had done so. The Franciscans could then help him transplant the remaining uncontaminated seeds of Christianity to this American garden, where they would, he hoped, take root and thrive.

In retrospect, it is both ironic and tragic that the same Franciscan mystic who believed that this Eden and its inhabitants were unspoiled and uncorrupted would also be the one to initiate their "conversion," their desecration, and their destruction. This discrepancy between intent and result was similar to discrepancies with which Saint Francis himself had grappled three centuries earlier, though clearly in a more humble manner than that taken by his latter-day follower, Columbus.

Like Columbus, Francis was not only a man of contradictions but a wayfarer as well. Restless and distraught that the Catholic empire had become depraved and degenerate, he journeyed far and wide for someone of his time, from Spain to the Crusades in the Holy Lands. In the fervor of his youth, he wandered around trying to convert the masses, urging them to take the vows of poverty, to abandon their worldly possessions, their families, and their adherence to the formalities of the church.

But there came a time when he realized the folly of converting people in a way that cut them off from their families, their crafts, and their traditional life-styles. In Cannara, just a few miles from Assisi, Francis began to preach among a bunch of rough-edged peasants: spelt farmers, millstone cutters, wicker weavers, woodcutters, and ox drivers. They hardly stopped their work when he first began to proselytize, but when they saw that a flock of swallows had settled down to listen to him, their diffidence fell away. Immediately, every last man and woman set their tools down to join Francis in his life of poverty and celibacy. It then dawned on him that he was asking them to forsake all the relationships with one another and with their plants, animals, and lands that they had ever known. As the Assisi historian, Fortini, tells it:

> Without regret, they would leave their beloved homes, their warm hearths, the walls they had fought over, the clear water of the river, their moist furrows, their flocks and herds. All were ready to forget, just as in the hour of dying, their work, their

affections, hopes and memories, their seeding and harvesting, their
mills, meadowlands and woodlands, the soothing sound in the long
night hours of a shuttle on the loom. . . . Joining Francis in his
mission was more important than their loves and marriages, their
tender little ones and white-haired old men and the dead asleep
in the church. . . . Francis's heart was shaken by this heroic self-
offering of a whole people. What was he to do?

He told them to remain true to what they did best, to
remain in their cultural community, their environmental context. "Don't be in a hurry and don't leave," he said, and
thus they stayed amid the forested hills, the willow-choked
swamps, and the canebrakes of Cannara.

A few years later, in 1221, not far from Florence, Francis
came upon a solution to the dilemma first posed for him at
Cannara. An old man named Lucchesio heard Francis preach
and impulsively gave away everything he had to the poor,
leaving his wife with only a small garden and a ramshackle
home. His elderly wife then agreed to be converted as well.
However, while they were taking the vows of poverty, they
broke down, unable to imagine going their separate ways.
They began to plead with Francis to let them stay together,
for they would surely die if they could no longer rely on one
another. It was then that he conceived of a secular order of
Franciscans, who could maintain their traditional ways of life
as long as they refrained from bearing arms, from hatred,
and from taking oaths in support of feuding powers. Rather
than wrenching country people from their deepest connections with the world, Francis came to accept the dignity of
a "life in place." His own concept of conversion, from *con-*

vertire, "to turn around," spun back on itself and was put to rest.

As the train to Rome rolled on through drizzling rain, past small groups of lights that indicated towns and through periodic darkness, I gauged my own life's trajectory against those of Francis and Columbus. I was obviously no saint nor any sort of discoverer, but in my early career I had shared a measure of missionary zeal with these two men. I had wanted everyone to become born-again environmentalists. I had preached that agriculture had degenerated in its use of land and plants, and accordingly, that it required an overhaul through an infusion of new genes from wild species. Thus, I took seeds from one indigenous community to another, whose traditional planting stock had been lost. I transplanted ideas, images, and values from one culture to another. I tried to reconstruct Eden in the form of some perfect relationship between the human community and the unspoiled desert community, but I never got to live in such a relationship because I was too busy running around proselytizing.

Ultimately, I saw my own relationships unravel rather than strengthen—not only my relationship with my former wife but also those with some of my friends—and I lost whatever rooted sense of place I had been able to find. I worried as seeds that I loved fell into the hands of plant breeders and entrepreneurs who had no respect for the plants' original context. I gradually lost interest in being involved in further plant exploration, if it meant extracting seeds from their natural and cultural habitats only to see them manipulated, patented, and commercialized while local gene pools evaporated and traditional farmers went belly up. I had reached a time in my life when I not only felt the weight of my failed marriage but of my former career as well.

I heard the train whistle blow as we approached some Italian village whose name flashed by too fast for me to read. I closed my eyes, sad and tired. The conversations in the seats around me had waned; the other passengers were dropping off to sleep. I could no longer hear Italian or German or French voices, only the clack of the steel wheels as they beat their weight against each successive set of rails on the line toward central Italy. Out of this rhythmic clatter and shuffle, I heard the pulsing beat of some twelve-bar blues: train songs lodged deep in my memory. The rhythms grew stronger; sometimes they slowed, at other times they sped up or shifted, but old-time blues trains kept on rolling through my head: Howlin' Wolf's *Smokestack Lightnin'*, Leadbelly's *Midnight Special*, Bukka White's *Special Steam Line*, and various versions of *Mystery Train*.

I must have fallen asleep hypnotized by the clack of the wheels on the train tracks and the lonesome moans of the whistle. When I awoke, the lights had come on in the passenger cars, and they were slowing to a stop at the Stazione Termini in the heart of Rome. The station was nearly deserted, except for bands of begging Gypsies and one lone German hippie panhandler, playing songs for spare change. He sat on a stool, facing away from us, but I could see that his Vagabond jeans were torn and dusty; his dirty blond hair fell down across his face and over the guitar. He was blowing into a harmonica wired in front of his mouth, banging out chords, and beating one boot against the ground, as everyone passed him by without tossing a single lira his way. When I realized that he was playing some European version of the blues, I stopped, reached into my change purse, and gave him a few lire, some pesos left over from my most recent trip to Mexico, and my last quarter. He didn't look up, just kept on playing. I flagged down a taxi and headed to the apartment of my Spanish friend Pepé, where I would stay less than a day, rearranging my bags before boarding a train for Florence.

Chapter 2

Someday, facing a world become more arid or once more taken over by trees, no one will realize how much intelligence man added to the forms of the earth by erecting the monuments of Florence amid the vast motions of the olive trees of Tuscany.

ANDRÉ MALRAUX

Florentine Treasures:
Campanilismo and the Conservers of Local Fruits

ost Americans come to Florence as art lovers, to see Michelangelo's *David*. I came instead as a pilgrim, to rendezvous with Ginger Harmon's smile and to prepare for tramping the road of Saint Francis. As it turned out, I also stopped to see vegetables, and to admire the fruity world of Bartolomeo Bimbi.

In Florence, it was easy to realize why I was no Renaissance man. When I had time to view fine art, I skipped the long lines in front of the masterpieces and darted out to a near-deserted villa in order to absorb the Medici gardens and the Bimbi portraits of pears and cherries. I was reminded of that innocent abroad, Mark Twain, with his irreverent view of Italian art history:

> I wish to say one word about Michael Angelo Buonarroti. I used to worship the mighty genius of Michael Angelo—that man who was great in poetry, painting, sculpture, architecture—great in everything he undertook. But I do not want Michael Angelo for breakfast—for luncheon—for dinner—for tea—for supper—for between meals. I like change, occasionally. In Genoa, he designed everything; in Milan, he or his pupils designed everything; he designed the Lake of Como; in Padua, Verona, Venice, Bologna, who did we ever hear of from guides but Michael Angelo? In Florence, he painted everything, designed everything, nearly, and what he did not design he used to sit on a favorite stone and look at, and they showed us the stone. . . . Dan said the other day to the guide, "Enough, enough, enough! Say no more! Lump the whole thing! Say that the Creator made Italy from designs by Michael Angelo!"
>
> I never felt so fervently thankful, so soothed, so tranquil, so filled with a blessed peace, as I did yesterday when I learned that Michael Angelo was dead.

I too have had chronic trouble with famous places. When I find myself coming to such places, it is for all the wrong reasons. Around the Casbah, I bypassed stores of jewelry, rugs, and Muslim religious art in order to buy American Indian sunflower seeds from a Moorish ·confectioner and to argue with shopkeepers over which were the best of the olive varieties that were curing in their salt-stained barrels. In Puerto Vallarta, Mexico, I stayed away from beaches and spent my time in the tropical forest collecting perennial beans; when I returned to my hotel room, I took a shower with half a dozen giant bean roots, to wash the mud off them and prepare them for planting in a nursery. Perhaps I became a plant explorer only to have an excuse for my socially inappropriate behavior.

In that way, I am not unlike Francesco di Bernardone, who showed up at the Vatican in rags, begging to have an audience with the pope. And earlier, when he renounced his own father, a garment merchant, he had taken off all his clothes in front of an assembly of citizens and the bishop of Assisi. I cannot imagine what Saint Francis would do in the face of the fashion centers of northern Italy, were he alive today.

I arrived in Florence as a blood-orange sun faded into the gray haze of the Tuscan sky. Out the window of my inn, I could see a sea of red tile roofs, rain-stained walls of cream, rust, and sienna, smokestacks, chimneys, antennae, and satellite dishes. Inside, I felt the fatigue of having flown around too much lately, of having become more accustomed to the cosmopolitan interiors of airports and train stations than to the land itself. It is odd that we consider "privileged" those who have become so detached from their family obligations and home that they are "free" to go anywhere. After two years of psychological disjunction and domestic crisis, what I wanted most out of the world was connection, not independence. Arriving tired and disoriented in a large city in a foreign country offered me little comfort, only further confirmation that I had strayed too far from my family, my home.

These pangs of self-doubt were followed by a bodily urge to get my feet back on the ground. I scrambled down the three flights of hotel stairs, ran out into the street, then down to the stones, mud, and weeds of a riverside park. Watching the flow of water was like a salve, washing over and softening the rough spots in my life. My eyes followed the currents, bobbed with the ducks, and rafted downstream with leaves and sticks. I was not home, but at least I felt alive once more.

I felt an inclination to walk, and walk I did. Fortunately, I had a destination in mind. Tuscan food authority Faith Willinger had invited me to come over the bridge, pass around a few corners, up some stairs, and into the kitchen where she deals daily with the raw and the cooked.

Faith has been in Florence enough years and has read enough of what foreigners write about Italian cuisine to know that her current project of interviewing just one old man was a bit of a gamble.

"I am simply spending time with one farmer who grows most of his own food, who eats meat only sparingly, who makes modest but piquant sauces, and who seldom provides me with recipes longer than a few lines. This is not haute cuisine; this is just delicious peasant cookery."

It is delicious, in part, because of the fresh texture and flavor of the vegetables that Torquato selects for his table. First he chooses the seeds he grows with great care, taking the majority of them from the best of the produce he has harvested over the years. He then plants a garden large enough to feed himself and to sell the surplus at Piazza Santo Spirito several days each week of the growing season. For his own table, he picks most of the greens immediately prior to preparing them. For the market, most of his produce arrives less than half a day after the picking, and it looks far more turgid and colorful than the same kinds found with other vendors.

Beginning with such ingredients, his homemade food has a distinctive edge over dishes dependent on foodstuffs precociously picked, sprayed with preservatives, and shipped between countries or even continents. But Torquato's rigor may be Willinger's downfall when she comes to promoting her unique cookbook, for her readers will be hard-pressed to find raw materials of comparable quality. This has made Faith nervous, but she has continued to devote her energies to recording every comment Torquato offers about Tuscan foods.

"I just don't know," Faith puzzled. "It's a risk. But perhaps it will make people realize where good food comes from. In any case, you must go to see Torquato tomorrow morning. He is always among the first to put out his vegetables in the market."

My friend Ginger arrived that night after bicycling through the Chianti region; seeing her energetic little body and sparkling grin again warmed my lonesome heart. We had stories to catch up on that wine and pasta could complement. We had plans to make, maps to scan, and alternate routes to consider. By the time we went back to our rooms to sleep, all the logistical details we had decided on were swirling in my head. I dreamed of walking across maps much of the night.

The next morning, Ginger was more than willing to forestall the museums for a few hours at a farmers' market. At the first stall, a four-foot-tall clump of wild sunflowers and a stack of Hubbard squash greeted us. We looked for the table of produce that belonged to Torquato. Faith had shown me a snapshot of the man in passing, but we had been so engaged in the description of vegetables that I had not asked for a better description of him.

Just then, Ginger solved the dilemma. "That must be him, from what you said. Look at the way he is arranging his produce. It all looks handpicked and delightful."

I turned my attention to the man Ginger had pointed out, and he vaguely fit the snapshot image that Faith had flashed by me. But the photo had captured an elderly man as a still life, while in the flesh this farmer-vendor was so animated.

"Che bello!" we exclaimed, admiring his vegetables.

"All of these come from my own land," he said proudly. He looked around, then quietly added, "Some of the others here, they will try to resell you what they buy at the big commercial market. Mine come straight from the earth and are still fresh when I arrive here at seven in the morning. Look at them closely, you'll see."

Now I had no doubt that we had found Signore Torquato. We introduced ourselves, and then he drew our attention back to the fresh produce. One by one, he told us the names and qualities of his vegetables.

"I call this *pomodoro ricco fiorentino*, a local variety that I have grown for a long time." It was a small, squat, wavy-ribbed tomato with a deep red color, bursting at its seams with juice.

"Is it sweet?" Ginger asked.

"Sweet? Well, it's sweet enough to eat fresh as a piece of fruit."

A fruit it was, and delicious as a ripe plum. Such qualities in a tomato are easily forgotten now that most of the ones we consume come puréed, stewed, or strained into sauces. In fact, the use of tomatoes in vegetable sauces and stews did not appear in Italian recipes until the 1692 publication of *Lo Scalco alla Moderna* by Antonio Latini. Torquato grows this tomato expressly for eating as a fruit and then grows others that are better suited for sauces. As he showed us his tomatoes, I remembered the story of their arrival and adoption in Italy.

Although Mexican crop seeds of this South American native were brought to Europe in the early 1500s, they were initially considered just another lovely, deadly nightshade. Giacomo Castelvetro's 1614 account of vegetables in Italy fails to mention them as part of the cuisine of that time. As late as 1666, a Genoese publication by Dominicus Chabraeus lumped them with other poisonous and malignant fruits. Gradually, however, tomatoes began to be seen as acrid New World analogues to eggplants and were given the eggplant's former nickname: *pomo di moro*, or fruit of the Moors, a term now contracted into *pomodoro*. For years, English historians have erroneously translated this term as "apples of love," perhaps wishfully thinking that they had aphrodisiacs at their disposal.

The earliest recorded Italian trials in cooking with tomatoes simply treated them like eggplants, slicing them, then frying them in olive oil with salt and pepper. Still, few were convinced of their merits. The *Herbo Nuovo* of naturalist Castor Durante rejected them, claiming that compared with true eggplants, they "scarcely provide the poorest of nourishment."

Then, in 1692, Latini challenged Italians to use tomatoes

in sauces, as was the current fashion in Spain. Apparently, this spurred some experimentation, because Padre Francesco Gaudentio published a tomato sauce recipe in his 1705 treatise on Tuscan cookery. He suggested "taking the tomatoes, cutting them into pieces, putting them in a pan with oil, salt, chopped garlic, and wild savory . . . adding a few soft breadcrumbs if you like."

While Torquato's Tuscan ancestors probably did not become tomatomaniacs until late in the last century, it was good to know that some Florentines still remember how fine *pomodori* taste as fresh, unadulterated fruits. They need not be sun-dried, sliced, squashed, stewed, or sautéed to be edible. But now, Torquato was moving our attention away from the tomato juice dripping down our chins toward another New World introduction that had endeared itself to him.

"This is my *zucca*," he said, blushing a little as he held a tender young squash in his hands. He motioned us closer, then whispered, "Not too many people here in the city understand that the *zucca*, she is feminine, and that the masculine part of the plant produces only flowers with pollen."

This was one of the few American vegetables already well accepted in Italy by 1614; Castelvetro knew how to fry, stew, and candy them when they emerged "right at the end of the scorching season." While the tender growth tips were used in a manner similar to those of bottle-gourd calabashes from Africa and Sicily, the Mexican custom of cooking squash blossoms did not arrive at the same time as the zucchini themselves.

Torquato held up his largest squashes, winked at us, then continued to show us his inventory. Ginger and I purchased sprigs of fresh basil, plum tomatoes fit for sauces, *rucola* greens, garden rocket salad, and a cayenne-sized chile that Torquato called *peperoncini di guazza*, or dewdrop pepper.

Torquato gathered up a handful of these peppers and spoke of his attraction to them: "This *peperoncini*, I take it and fry it with olive oil and garlic when I want something spicy-hot. The *piccante* is satisfying."

I had with me seed packets of a Mexican *chile del árbol*, which I gave to him. I commented on the obvious: "If these peppers do well here, you can save the seeds. You keep your own seeds, don't you?"

"Seeds? Of course I save them." He held up the Florentine tomato once again. "This comes from my seed—you can't get this kind from a rack in a store."

That was reassuring, for I was afraid that the Common Market seed trade regulations had put pressures on farmers to abandon the saving and replanting of hand-selected seeds. A European convention called the Union for the Protection of New Varieties of Plants (UPOV) has prohibited any farmers from selling seeds gleaned from their own crops as long as the ultimate source of those seeds was once purchased. The agribusinesses supporting UPOV claim that the regulations ensure the quality of seeds on the market and provide incentives for plant breeders to develop new, higher-yielding varieties for patenting. However, such prohibitions may ultimately function to reduce the diversity of vegetables in gardens and fields and to keep the profits of seed trade in the hands of a few.

I was also aware that European companies do a better job of breeding, packaging, and marketing vegetable seeds for home gardeners than their American counterparts do. They have an enormous market in southern Europe, for the portion of the population that religiously plants gardens has remained high. In nearly every town, garden seed racks are conspicuously displayed in corner grocery and hardware stores, on plazas, and particularly in open-air markets.

Nonetheless, place-specific crop varieties remain valued as well. Many a farmers' market displays locally favored vegetable, legume, and fruit varieties not found even in the nearest town. Names of completely different historical derivation may be used to distinguish two like-appearing vegetables that maintain different flavors and cooking properties even when cooked under identical conditions. Over five thousand folk names for field and garden crop varieties have been recorded in Italy, yet agronomists admit that they have done no more than document the tip of this horticultural iceberg. Five thousand crop names form a respectable lexicon for a country the size of Italy. For all its tribes of Indian farmers, I doubt whether Arizona has more than six hundred indigenous names for crop varieties within an area roughly the same size as Italy.

Such names often represent different notions about the origins of a crop. For example, consider the various names in Italian dialects for the New World introduction commonly known as maize: *granoturco*, Turkish corn; *formentone indiano*, Indian wheat, or frumenty; and simply, *siciliano*, the Sicilian crop. Origins aside, sometimes a plant's shape has captured the Italian imagination. The North American introduction of sunflowers has engendered a diversity of names: *girasole*, sun turner; *coppa di sole*, cup of sun; *corona reale*, royal crown; *tazza reggia*, regal cup; *mirasole*, sun-watcher; *pianta massima*, giant plant; and *eliotrope*, sun follower. It is ironic that so many of these names refer to the plants' responses to solar movements, because until the last decade, certain American botanists doubted what we now know as a certainty: that *Helianthus* leaves and flowers can actually track the sun's angles for photosynthetic gains. Italian farmers must have observed that sunflowers are solar trackers soon after their introduction, and improvised names to reflect this characteristic. This present use of so many local terms suggests that farmers prefer to retain locally coined terms rather than adopt the names bandied about in newspapers and agronomists' pamphlets.

But this linguistic pluralism is not limited to recent arrivals. Apricots, for instance, are an ancient Mediterranean orchard crop, one of several candidates for *the* forbidden fruit in the Garden of Eden. Nevertheless, apricots are hailed by at least thirteen aliases in Italy, ranging from the common *albicocca*, to *biricoccola*, to *meliaca* and *pesca armenica*.

Naming, in cases such as these, is one more means of endearment or of emotional possession of a crop. I realized this when I spotted a tomato similar to Torquato's *pomodoro ricco fiorentino* in another vendor's display.

"How do you say the name of this variety of *pomodoro*?" I asked.

"*Pomodoro rosso nostrale*," she declared, "our native red tomato." Then she added, "It is found in no other place."

The sentiment underlying this local possessiveness of distinctive crops, foods, and customs is known in Italy as *campanilismo*. It is somewhat negatively defined in dictionaries as "an excessive attraction to one's own homeland or birthplace." As it is derived from the word for bell, *campana*, a more literal definition might be "belief or faith in what lies within earshot of the village bell."

This provincialism certainly has its detractors, but it is not the same as myopia. At its core is a heartfelt appreciation for local resources and traditions. This appreciation has fostered the rich cultural, agricultural, and culinary heritage that has characterized much of rural Italy, as well as many other peasant cultures around the world.

Tuscans express a certain distrust of foods produced beyond their province, or more accurately, beyond their sphere of familiarity. If they do not produce their own olive oil, they will endeavor to purchase a significant quantity from a relative or neighbor. Otherwise, they cannot be sure that the olives were properly grown, harvested, pressed, and processed without being adulterated. One Tuscan was only half-joking when he dismissed my questions about foods available in an Umbrian valley less than thirty miles away. He snapped at me, "Don't ask us about what they might cook over there. For all we know, they may eat dogs!"

Such an attitude has kept Signore Torquato's farmers' market healthy. After we said good-bye to Torquato, we wandered around the other stands, listening to customers grill the vendors about the freshness and origin of each possible purchase. They haggled over spiny cucumbers, round eggplants, serpentine cowpeas, and Florence fennel. They fingered open the cranberry-colored pods of *fagioli borgati*, hamlet beans, pinched the muscadine grapes, and eyed the green figs. Ginger noticed a crowd forming around an enormous cylindrical squash, related to butternut and the big cheese pumpkins.

"I've never seen anything like it before!" she exclaimed.

A blond Australian with a punk razor cut overheard our English and entered the conversation. "Are you commenting on that pumpkin? Isn't it beautiful? You know, I cooked up a pumpkin for the Brits when I worked outside of London as a domestic, and damn them, they wouldn't eat it! They say it is only good for feeding to livestock. Or worse, some Brits claim that only *ethnic* people would stoop to eat anything like that! I swear, they wouldn't ever put a single bloody vegetable in their mouths if they could get away with it!"

There was a time, of course, when such garden oddities captured the attention of all of Europe. As Italo Calvino describes in *The Baron in the Trees*, possession of such rare vegetables once lent status to families such as the Ondarivas of Ombrosa; Calvino comments on "the jealous care which the Ondarivas took of their garden, full, it was said, of the rarest plants. In fact, the grandfather of the present Marquis had been a pupil of the botanist Linnaeus, and since his time all the family connections at the courts of France and England had been set in motion to send the finest botanical rarities from the colonies. For years boats had unloaded at the port of Ombrosa sacks of seeds, bundles of cuttings, potted shrubs, and even entire trees with huge wrappings of sacking around the roots; until the garden—it was said—had become a mixture of the plants of India and the Americas, and even of New Holland."

Such a scene could well have been placed at the Medici summer villas just outside Florence. Grand Duke Cosimo III and Prince Ferdinando de' Medici were such avid collectors of botanical and zoological monstrosities that they filled building after building with specimens and paintings. While few of the progeny of their living collections survived Florence's turbulent political climate of the last three centuries, their images have survived in the oil paintings of Bartolomeo Bimbi.

It was serendipitous that Bimbi eventually came to match the Medicis' fervor for natural history with his own for still life. For the first two decades of his career, he was content with painting copies of famous portraits, architectural decorations, and grotesques for various Florentine houses. Then, while visiting a friend's studio, he was thunderstruck by the beauty captured in a garland of flowers painted larger than life. He immediately returned home and began devoting his time to painting flowers and fruits.

Soon Prince Ferdinando de' Medici began to send Bimbi the rarest and most striking flowers or fruits that came into his collection so that his paintings might preserve them for posterity. Ferdinando and Cosimo III then enlisted him as the official documentary artist of their burgeoning menagerie of biological oddities. At that time, precursors of natural history museums emphasized the unnatural mutant or monster more than the typical plant. Bimbi, however, kept his focus on the diversity of forms that one species of fruit could take, thus providing a context even for the oddities. At the same time, Cosimo III became such a compulsive collector that he built a lovely new villa largely to house his rustic gene bank. Cosimo's biographer Baldinucci, a contemporary and friend of Bimbi, describes the Medici project in this manner: "[Topaia is] situated at the summit of the famous vineyards of the royal villa of Castellon, and since this place was and still is full of every kind of fruit tree, including citrus fruits, grapes, and flowers known hitherto, . . . he wished that it also be adorned with *natura morta* [still life] paintings representing the same."

Like the wild mountain hermitage given to Francis at La

Verna by Count Orlando, the known world of domesticated plants was placed at Bartolomeo Bimbi's beck and call by the Medicis. I have always found it curious that some of the most creative painters, poets, and spiritual misfits of Europe were patronized by the royalty of the time. It is ironic that the few glimpses we have of natural diversity as it existed in medieval Europe remain, for the large part, due to royal families wealthy and confident enough not to be threatened by this diversity and its attendant "free spirits."

Later that day, Ginger and I made our way out to the hamlet of Poggio a Caiano, where one of the "beautiful little villas" of the Medicis imposed itself on the hillside like a fortress of fortune. This mansion-turned-art-gallery does not pull the crowds that a dozen other galleries around Florence attract. In fact, as we entered, I could see no one at the gate or in the gardens. When we finally passed indoors, the three caretakers walked us through each room of the entire mansion. They made perfunctory stops in front of each significant painting and repeated, "Very beautiful, isn't it?" as if performing some aesthetic equivalent of the stations of the cross.

Fortunately for us, the celebration of a recent International Horticultural Congress in Florence had moved the locals to dust off many of Bimbi's paintings that had been languishing in storage. What struck me about them was the artist's mania for capturing the botanical details of the fruits that were his subjects—fruits that have seldom been seen, let alone studied, in this century. Bimbi would simply plop down three dozen kinds of cherries on the same green velvet background, then go after every subtle hue, sheen, shape, or size difference among them. This was not a man content with using a prefabricated "cherry red" tint, if such a thing happened to be in his paintbox. To his eye, each cherry was worlds apart from the others.

Bimbi did not stop at cherries. By 1720, he had painted 12 kinds of apricots, 39 different plums, 36 peaches, 52 types of apples, 74 grape varieties, 88 sorts of citrus, 106 pears, and 51 types of figs. Throw in his portraits of pumpkins, truffles, cauliflowers, and the ferocious wolf that terrorized local peasants, and Bimbi's art can be said to embody perfectly the proverb "Variety is the spice of life."

While looking at hundreds of his painted fruits, carefully rendered and discreetly labeled, Ginger and I felt a certain wonder that so much diversity had been brought together at one time in one place. Whenever I am exposed to the visual and tactile pleasures of natural or cultural diversity, I feel as though I've arrived at my version of heaven.

In this case, my delight was gradually replaced by the sad realization that many of the varieties that Bimbi had immortalized are no longer available anywhere that we know. I must have been visibly moved by this realization, because Ginger asked me if I was okay.

"Oh, Ginger, I'm just sad. A lot of this splendid diversity is now gone. I've always thought of Europe as a biologically poor place, but now I see that it wasn't always that way. How many of its living riches have been swept away by wars, famine, disease, or just plain neglect?"

"But, Gary, that's history as we have known it," Ginger replied. "It has been hard enough for the Italians to preserve their most famous paintings and architectural monuments through all their economic and political ups and downs.

You're talking about something infinitely more difficult to save, aren't you?"

"I suppose I am," I sighed. "I'm talking of a society having the forethought to support generation after generation of horticulturalists and nature sanctuary wardens in order to preserve living resources from one century to the next. And that would take valuing diversity and wildness as much as they obviously have valued fine art."

"If you had seen the poverty and degraded conditions here in 1951, as I did—when I could see costs of World War II everywhere, on every street—you'd be amazed at how much the Italians have managed to preserve of their heritage."

"I suppose you're right," I conceded. "It's to their credit that there are as many Italians as there are today concerned with conserving diversity."

I soon met one of those Italians. While Ginger was occupied with other pursuits, I called on Giannozzo Pucci, a true Renaissance man from nearby Fiesole. Pucci has cast a cultural net over Tuscany to catch the remaining riches from Bimbi's time. Once a year, Pucci and his friends sponsor La Fierucola, a revival of an ancient agricultural fair once held in the vicinity of Florence. Seed swappers, fruit growers, nursery owners, potters, and other self-employed artisans come to sell or trade their wares. Pucci has also promoted smaller agricultural fairs adjacent to established farmers' markets as opportunities for local people to exchange traditional seeds and agricultural knowledge.

At first, these fairs were largely attended by young people who have gone back to the land to grow food according to biodynamic or organic methods. Over the last eight years, however, more and more of the peasant farmers of Torquato's ilk have joined in La Fierucola. A May fair in the hillside hamlet of Pistoia, for example, has achieved moderate success in an area where there are fewer young people but many elderly farmers. Nevertheless, Giannozzo is not overly optimistic about the prospects of capturing the remaining range of heirloom fruits and vegetables.

"Many will disappear very soon," he lamented. "Such seeds will die with the old people. That is because the distinctive seeds are entwined with certain families or communities who save seeds at will—by heart, you might say —without thinking of the scientific or cultural value of the seeds."

Today, much of the extant vegetable diversity in Italy does not lie in the hands of the rich—the modern equivalents of the Medicis are the multinational genetic engineering corporations—but in the hands of the poor. As small landholders die or as economic changes force them off their parcels, this diversity is left behind in sheds and cellars that are ultimately cleaned out, torn down, or refurbished. The seeds and their stories lose their viability, and their passing goes virtually unnoticed.

That is why my friend in Rome, Dr. José "Pepé" Esquinas-Alcazar, calls them "orphan crops." That term would have appealed to Saint Francis, for his inclination always led him to work with what was neglected. That same inclination is strong in Pepé, who for decades worked in the field to conserve the vegetable diversity on several continents. He now coordinates the activities of the Food and Agriculture Organization's Commission on Plant Genetic Resources, a body affiliated with the United Nations. For all the hoopla he hears about historic preservation and the conservation of biological diversity, Pepé is not convinced that locally adapted minor crops are receiving the attention they deserve. He has observed that regional botanical gardens, provincial governments, and local agricultural schools set their sights on finer, more distant riches than those in their own backyards.

Giannozzo, for his part, has helped to plan an orphanage for these waifs. One of the Medici villas is being renovated and converted to serve as a meeting ground for those Italians who are experimenting with the time-tried agricultural traditions suited to their areas. Giannozzo's hope is that seeds as well as students will enter the villa's gates and nurture one another into something lasting. This time, the villa will leave for posterity more than just a few *natura morta* paintings. This time, he hopes, nature and culture will continue to live as cohabitants in a long and fruitful relationship.

Reunited back at the inn, Ginger and I added a supply of fruits and vegetables to our already burgeoning backpacks. We had tasted just a small bit of Florence but were now eager to leave it so that we could enter the country of Saint Francis. His hermitage on Monte La Verna, where he received the stigmata, was just a few hours away by bus. There we would begin our pilgrimage on foot. On our way to the bus station, I remembered a story about San Francesco that I wished I had shared with Signore Torquato.

The early Franciscans were a heterogeneous brotherhood, ranging from unschooled peasants to university professors well versed in the ultimate philosophical questions of their time. One of the latter was consumed by the dilemma of how to ensure himself an afterlife in heaven. This intellectual brother finally brought his anxieties to the attention of Francis. He asked the saint what he personally would do if he learned that the world was about to come to an end.

Francis did not pause a moment from the work in front of him. He answered, "I would continue hoeing and planting my garden."

When he could finally speak, the humbled philosopher turned to his companions and said, "My brothers, the theology of this man is a soaring eagle, while our learning crawls on its belly along the ground."

Interlude 2
Bus Ride to Monte La Verna

 e had walked, with backpacks loaded to the hilt, over to the bus station. We were to wait for a thirty-five-mile bus ride on the Passo della Consuma, east from Florence to Monte La Verna. But just as we put our packs down, I decided I didn't need as many field guides and as much plant-collecting gear on our hike. I ran some items back to storage in the hotel. When I returned, Ginger was smiling at me in a curious way.

"What did you leave *in* your bag? That's what I want to know."

"Well, I still have Huxley's *Fiori di Montagna*, a plant press, camera, binoculars, the field guide to European birds, and . . ."

"I've been meaning to ask you, Gary, are you taking all this with you because you will be doing some seed collecting or a full technical biological study along the way?"

I squirmed. "Well, I just want to be able to identify the plants and animals on the pilgrimage route . . ."

Ginger caught me: "But are you walking to study the land or to be a spiritual pilgrim of some kind?"

I grew a little defensive. "Well, I don't necessarily see any contradiction in terms . . ." Then I crumbled. "Ginger, I'm not sure. I mean, I'm *somewhere* between being an itinerant naturalist and a Franciscan pilgrim, but I don't know exactly where that is. My guess is that the land itself here is spirited and that it will inspire us in ways I can't predict now."

"Is Saint Francis one of those spirits?"

"Sure, I guess so, for me at least. San Francisco, wolves, doves, sacred mountains . . ." I could feel my rational arguments breaking down, going nowhere. The bus finally pulled up. Ginger and I climbed aboard and put our gear on the seats behind us. We headed out of town, along gardens lining the Arno River floodplain, following the stream to Pontassieve. We looked out the windows for a while, then resumed our conversation.

"Are you walking to Assisi as other Catholics do?" Ginger asked.

I shook my head. "I don't know if I'm doing it as they

do. They may feel the pull of Saint Francis, but maybe the wolves and the birds don't mean a thing to them. The trouble is, I feel this connection with the Franciscan tradition, but I don't really feel like a full-fledged Catholic, especially since my divorce. No rosary, no private confession, no disaffection for those who practice family planning. I didn't grow up with nuns rapping me over the knuckles or with priests assigning me penance. Like most Americans, I grew up in a world that was only covertly Christian, with an Irish Catholic mother and a Lebanese Lutheran father. I then began going to mass with O'odham friends and hiking to Saint Francis shrines. Later on, well, I ended up being the only pro-choice evolutionary biologist attending secular Franciscan meetings with the old guard of the order." I grimaced. "Oh, Ginger, it's all kind of messy . . ."

"Well, I don't think that's so different from the feelings that a lot of other people have about organized religion," Ginger said soothingly. "I know plenty of Jews who feel at home with Jewish customs and idioms but don't go to synagogue because institutionalized religion doesn't suit them. They fully embrace being Jewish *culturally* . . ."

"Judaic symbols probably loom large in their minds and ours no matter what," I offered.

"Sure. I have Jewish ancestry, but my parents didn't raise me as a Jew. I have an intellectual interest in my heritage but no deep emotional and spiritual connections to it."

"For me," I moaned, "part of the problem is my aversion to formal, rigid structures. Many of us in my generation are inherently uncomfortable with them, but I'm afraid that we're too apt to dismiss them categorically. As Wendell Berry told me, 'dispensing with formalities is one thing that forthright Americans are always proud to do.' I don't know, maybe there are some costs involved."

"Like what?"

"I don't know," I stammered. "Maybe . . . like divorces. The Catholic church maintains that we're apt to give up too quickly, to toss in the towel before the game is over. One of my Native American friends, Roxanne Swentzell, says the same thing. She said once, 'Western culture has this thing: if it gets hard, if life gets to be a struggle . . . just pack up and move. . . . It never really has to deal with problems. With traditional cultures, because they are tied to a spot, a family, and everything, somehow that's the *whole* world. You can't leave it . . . Whenever you hit a problem, you're going to have to go through it because you can't go anywhere. You are *at* the center of the world.' "

"I can see the value of that point of view. At one time or another, most of us have to make it through the dilemma of balancing freedom with cultural constraints."

"The eerie thing is, Ginger, I think I'm here because I empathize with how much of Francesco's life was spent dealing with that struggle—whether to stay or to move on. First he renounced his biological father and said that his only father was God, then he started to preach outside the conventions of the church. When he had gathered so many followers that he could have been burned as a heretic, he went to the pope and asked for permission to establish a new order. When conservatives decided that his mandates for his followers—voluntary poverty, no worldly possessions—were too restrictive, and they conveniently 'lost' the Rule that Francis had written, he finally acquiesced to a formal structure that was not to his personal liking. But when he saw how his own order was diverted and corrupted from carrying out his original vision during his lifetime, he resigned as a leader and spent much of the rest of his life in solitary meditation. It seems like his entire life was spent struggling with the conflict between honoring the formal traditions of his culture and questing for fresh expression. And I'm far worse at dealing with those dilemmas than he was."

"Maybe you needn't struggle so much," Ginger mused. "Leave some options open, remain calm and unharried in the face of all the variables presented to you, and surely you'll see a clear way through sooner or later. Let the way reveal itself."

"I've heard you say that before, Ginger." I smiled. "You must really mean it, don't you?"

We changed buses at Bibbiena, near the watershed divide between the two great rivers of the Etruscans, the Arno and the Tiber. From there on, our ride into the range of hills called the Alpi di Catenaia would be shrouded by clouds.

"I do mean it," Ginger said when we had sat down again. "What do you believe as a naturalist—as one who is near to but not quite *in* the Catholic tradition?"

"That we make our own heaven or hell here on this earth. It's all in how we live . . ."

"Nevertheless, you still wonder whether anyone in the Catholic church cares about this earth and Saint Francis the way you do?"

I sighed. "I don't really expect them to . . ."

"Does it matter?" Ginger asked, tilting her head so that she could hear my answer above the noise of the bus.

"Well, I suppose not." I frowned. "But is it appropriate

for me to ask if there are consequences to my having a different interpretation than the church about nearly everything on earth?"

Ginger broke into a laugh. "This reminds me of a game they used to play on the 'Steve Allen Show.' Steve Allen would say, 'Here's the answer. Now, what's the question?' "

Ginger paused, then began again. "I can agree that there surely are consequences, but I'm not certain that they have to be so worrisome. I can't quite imagine that the best balance between formality and creative expression in your own life will be exactly the same as what Francis chose, what the contemporary Catholic church endorses, or for that matter, what anyone else needs. I can't imagine that in all different contexts, the same answer fits every ethical question."

"Okay, okay." I smiled, giving in. "I'll try to let the way reveal itself."

The bus driver put on his brakes and slowed to a stop on a steep mountainside. La Verna towered above us.

Chapter 3

I don't know if it's true, the story they tell in books, that in ancient days a monkey could have left Rome and skipped from tree to tree until it reached Spain, without ever touching earth. The only place so thick in my day was the whole length . . . of Ombrosa and its valley right up to the mountain crests. . . . At one time, pines must have dominated the whole area, for a few tufts still sprouted here or there. . . . The oaks were far thicker than they seem today, for they were the first, most valuable victims. Higher up, the pines gave way to the chestnuts, which went on and up the mountainsides as far as the eye could reach. This was the world of sap amid which we lived, we inhabitants of Ombrosa, almost without noticing it.

ITALO CALVINO

La Verna's Wounds:
From Montane Sanctuary
to Chestnut Grove

onte La Verna was where we would start our sauntering in earnest, after a good night's sleep in a chalet-style lodge. Our third-story rooms, although without heat, were far more comfortable than the Sasso Spicco cave on the mountain that Francis first visited in 1213 and to which he would return for retreats five more times during the course of his life. This was where Francis spent forty days fasting in the

fall of 1224. While he prayed outside his cave on the night of September 14 of that year, the flesh of his hands and chest began to open and ooze with wounds, and he received a vision of being lanced and nailed to a cross. Villagers of nearby Chiusi della Verna still tell of what their ancestors saw that night: the summit of Monte La Verna was illuminated by an unearthly light, but no one immediately knew its origin. It was not until much later, when the companions of Francis saw his Christlike wounds, still oozing with the suffering of the crucifixion, that they guessed that the stigmata had been given to him that evening.

The mountain was not illuminated but shrouded in fog when Ginger and I arrived at the hillside village of Chiusi della Verna. We heard a chorus of mountain singing like that which Francis may have heard when he first ascended the peak with his brothers Masseo, Angelo, and Leo in 1213. As we began to climb the narrow trail up to La Verna's summit, I recalled the story of the songbirds that had welcomed Francis:

> When they were come nigh at the foot of the very rock of La Verna, it pleased Saint Francis to rest a while under an oak tree that stood by the way, and there standeth to this day; and resting beneath it Saint Francis began to consider the lay of the place and of the country round about. And lo, while he was thus pondering there came a great multitude of birds from divers parts that, with singing and fluttering of their wings, showed forth great joy and gladness, and surrounded Saint Francis, in such wise that some settled on his head, some on his shoulders, and some on his arms, some on his bosom, and some around his feet. His companions, beholding this, marveled greatly, and Saint Francis rejoiced in

spirit, and spake thus: "I do believe, dearest brothers, that it is pleasing to our Lord Jesus Christ that we abide on this solitary mountain, since our sisters and brothers the birds show forth such great joy at our coming."

The birds welcomed us, but so did birdshot in the distance. It was hunting season, and the sound of gunfire would stay with us throughout our trip, up until we celebrated the Feast of Saint Francis in Assisi. For the moment, however, no hunters were in sight, for the La Verna forest itself is a national monument where hunting is prohibited.

"Now I feel like we've begun," Ginger said as we climbed toward La Penna, the 3,800-foot precipice at the summit of La Verna. I could not answer her; I was panting and scanning the forest as we walked.

We climbed the ancient cobblestone path up through the oak, beech, and fir, rose hips, brambles, and ferns. The trail was an old one; in places, the cobbles had been buried by sediments moving down from open, eroded areas. In more protected spots, moss completely covered the limestones, the fence posts, and the trail markers. It was difficult to walk the trail without imagining Francis on the very same route. I spotted a white-haired, bent-over man, seated on a bench not far from the trailhead.

"Pardon me, but how far is it to La Penna?" I asked.

"Walking vigorously, fifteen minutes to the sanctuary and another fifteen to La Penna. Not so bad, eh? There is a paved road to the chapels and lodging where his cave was at the sanctuary, but you can stay on this little trail all the way up."

As the fog became thicker, we passed lichen-covered

wooden crosses, shrines, and little stone chapels. Then, suddenly, we were vaulted off the forest pathway and into a
huge parking lot serving no less than fifteen buildings
crouched around the original chapel of Santa Maria degli
Angeli. Some of the buildings were multistoried and enormous. I began to realize that my expectations had been naive,
particularly the one that the little hovels and caverns that
Francis had loved would have been kept free from Catholic
monument building. It did not matter to most visitors that
Francis had lived according to the Gospel's guidelines for
transients and faunal migrants: "Foxes have their holes and
birds have their roosts, but the Son of Man has nowhere to
lay his head." Francis himself had taken a dim view of the
followers who had not even waited for him to pass before
they began to erect monuments to him and to their cause,
taking over universities and grand monasteries. The La Verna
hermitage, I could see, was part of the same syndrome.

This complex of chapels, living quarters, and galleries
was wondrous in scale and splendor. La Verna focused not
only on Francis but also on other early Franciscans who were
later granted sainthood; Bonaventure and Anthony now had
their own separate chapels. The whole place was worked up
in stately gray stone, embellished with Della Robbia terra-
cotta. And it was all too much to behold; I failed to make
it past all the murals depicting the life of the saint, for the
corridor that they lined was as long and as intimidating as
any I had ever walked.

Instead, in less than half an hour, I succumbed to something akin to claustrophobia—or was it a fear of too much
sheen? All the rough edges of Francesco's life seemed worn
smooth and shiny by so many people passing by and polishing

his image. I longed to sense the dark, difficult, unembellished parts.

In that corridor, I could only see how Francesco and his poor brothers, among the first to take vows of voluntary simplicity, had been turned into celebrities and how their hovel-like chapels had become more like theaters or wax museums. Saturated, I impulsively walked up to the first door I saw and opened it, hoping to find a way out, perhaps a stairwell back to the trail. But that is not what I found.

There in front of me was a moss-covered grotto, luminous with the diffuse daylight that had filtered through the fog and rustling with a breeze that shook all the leaves in the trees above it. I did a double take: had I just entered an atrium? No, it was simply a room with no walls other than the mountainside, no ceiling other than the canopies of beeches, and no floor except the moss and decaying leaves.

"If Francesco were alive today, he would make this his quarters," I chuckled to myself. Then, another double take: when I had turned in a semicircle to scan the entire grotto, something caught my eye. Steps led down to a cave with a small sign beside its opening: "Letto de San Francesco." These *were* his quarters, the Sasso Spicco, his refuge during forty-day fasts and his inner sanctum where he fully faced his fears, doubts, and vagrant dreams.

I slipped behind a fence meant to keep visitors from banging their heads or stubbing their toes in the darkness of the grotto's fissures. I stepped down a few stairs into the shadows of the cave. There, I wedged myself between two rocks like a lizard, and let my pores absorb as much of that space—cold, dark, and musky—as they could. Regardless of the hour of the day, regardless of the fog, regardless even of the trees and the rock itself, the grotto's innermost space was not without light.

I remembered the words of Susan Saint Sing, who felt that it was no coincidence that Francesco had finally made peace with the world while nestled within the darkness of the earth: "Francis found something in his cave, something so profound and startling that his whole life was changed. . . . It was as tangible as a solid wall, yet at the same time as elusive as the fog. It kept his heart waiting. Then one day, it stayed and never left again."

This grotto was a cove at the edge of a sea of night fog. I came out of it with a sense of relief that the rustic cave of poor Francesco had not yet been buried beneath a gilded basilica. It was still possible to remember here, as Franciscan Murray Bodo wrote, that Francis sought out "lonely places." Why? "To burrow into the earth in search of a treasure which lies hidden from those who live only on the surface." Perhaps I too was walking a lonesome highway to seek out such hollows; the hollowness that I felt inside after my divorce needed to be met in its darkest depths, not painted over on the surface to make everything look fine.

I found Ginger, and we walked up the trail past the walled enclosure of the hermitage, following a ridge that would, on most days, have provided an overview of the surrounding valleys and mountains. Today, because it was fogged in, it gave us no better sense of where we would be going. "That's okay," said Ginger, flashing one of her large, lovely smiles that would continue to endear her to me over the course of our pilgrimage together. "The way will reveal itself," she said, partly in parody of the conversation we had had the day before but mostly in true enthusiasm for whatever came along.

As we ascended through the mists above the hermitage and groped our way along La Spina della Verna, we began to notice one floral signpost after another assuring us that we were on the right trail. Wherever the brown-robed brothers had erected shrines, statues, or stations of the cross, someone had recently come along and placed in their midst small bouquets of cyclamen—or *panporcino*, as cyclamen is called here. It is a carmine-colored primrose whose twisted petals unfurl as they open, like an umbrella. Also as they open, they release a perfume that pervades the air around them for several yards. I loved the way these hardy little plants offered such color and fragrance to an otherwise muted world. They would show up again later on our pilgrimage, and again they would be in a special place.

Soon we had climbed to the top of La Verna's forest, where we could encounter beech, fir, ash, and oak of enormous girths. Always a tree hugger, even I was overwhelmed here: I gave one of these giants four consecutive embraces as I moved around its circumference, and I still had not come full circle. Forest historian J. V. Thirgood has seen this phenomenon of large relictual trees elsewhere in forests long associated with saints: "The marked difference in the plant cover of sacred ground—cemeteries, shrines, and marabouts—[as opposed to] adjacent profane ground, may be seen in most Mediterranean countries. . . . In such protected situations, there are differences in the composition and density of plant formations, and in the height and girth of trees."

I had hoped that such dignified trees would still be standing at La Verna, although I knew that most of the Tuscan forests had not fared well over the last six centuries. In 1849, Giuseppe del Noce compared Tuscan records of fifteenth-century forests with similar records newly placed in his hands. Over those four and a half centuries, most of the major tree species in Tuscany had seen their numbers reduced by 20 percent.

Yet in just the century and a half since Giuseppe del Noce's reckoning, an equal number of trees have been lost from the Tuscan countryside, for fields and pastures have been mechanically cleared on hills earlier thought to have been too soil-poor and precipitous to serve farmers and herders. Other wooded mountainsides have remained too difficult to work, but even so, no more than 60 percent of the forests that were known in Tuscany during the days of Francis persist today.

Sacred groves like those at La Verna and those above Assisi on Subasio are reputedly among the last holdouts in this region. Such forest enclaves have been spared for spiritual rather than economic or ecological reasons. And they are highly esteemed precisely because they provide a clear contrast to the widespread deforestation around them.

On an earlier trip to Italy, I had mentioned to the World Wildlife Fund's Gianfranco Bologna that I was curious about the relictual plant diversity left on La Verna and Subasio. He had kindly cautioned me: "If you are expecting La Verna to be a good area of wildness, you will be disappointed. It is a good place for meditation, but it is not biologically rich anymore like the Carceri forest on Monte Subasio . . . They are such small forests compared to what you might be used to in the Americas."

Ecologists like Bologna rightly recognize that the biological diversity of any forest is not merely related to how long a place has been preserved; it also reflects the size and habitat heterogeneity of the place. If similar forests are not too far away or if they are linked by corridors through which plants and animals can "migrate," diversity has a better chance of being sustained. La Verna may have included some of Tuscany's original vegetation, for it had never fallen beneath the plow. Nevertheless, the forest is hardly large enough or close enough to other kindred forests to retain much variety within and beneath its canopy.

I had hoped that the sacred mountains of Saint Francis would be refuges of biological diversity, but I could not tell for sure whether that was true here at La Verna. I would take up the same concern when I had more botanizing time on my hands at Monte Subasio, after Ginger and I had arrived in Assisi.

Now we began a blind descent from La Verna. Whether the Tiber valley were immediately below us or whether a mountain range rose between us and the valley, we had no way of knowing, for the landscape remained steeped in thick fog. We moved along as one does in pitch-black darkness, hoping to grab onto some tangible object and then feel our way forward.

Within the first half-mile, I made out a tree vaguely familiar to me, although it looked more like an upright shadow than a green, growing being. I eyed its large, saw-toothed, lance-shaped leaves. I might have seen it in some book before, but I was not certain that I had ever seen it growing in the ground.

"Ginger! Let's stop for a moment. I need to look this one up, even though its name seems on the tip of my tongue."

I unhitched the belts of my backpack and let its weight drop to my feet. I untied the top flap and rummaged through the pockets of the smaller knapsack inside where I was keeping a field guide to help me identify trees.

All the while, Ginger stood patiently with her pack still on, staring at the wet ground beneath her feet. Finally she asked, "Which tree are you trying to identify? *This* one with all the chestnuts underneath?"

I smiled, looking up at the tree, then down at the mound of nuts on the ground. I put the field guide away without even opening it. The European chestnut needed no more confirmation than its fruit.

While its identity was easy, I wasn't sure if it had been intentionally planted or had sprung up as part of the spontaneous roadside vegetation. That uncertainty, like others on this trip, would have taken an intimate knowledge of local history to resolve. I had no such knowledge, but I assumed that chestnuts had been moved around by humans for so long that their presence in this particular spot must reveal social as much as natural history. This chestnut had been a native to Europe prior to the arrival of human cultures but had disappeared from southern Europe during the Ice Age and taken refuge in southwest Asia. Prehistoric planters carried it out of eastern Turkey into Anatolia and Greece more than 3,500 years ago. They returned it to Italy, where it proliferated with the help of the human hand. Even those trees in Italian landscapes that look the wildest, even those in places unmanipulated by humans for decades, are among the most domesticated of all chestnuts in the Mediterranean region, for they did not arrive in Italy as wildlings but were fully domesticated by the time they were dispersed from eastern Turkey to the Apennines thousands of years ago.

As Ginger and I ambled onward, I noticed chestnuts tucked into every possible context: roadside hedges, dense forests of towering trees, orchardlike plantations of several acres, abandoned barnyards, and village plazas where no other trees were planted.

We continued on through drizzle and fog, coming across little traffic on the road except for herds of sheep being moved from one pasture to another. All the while, we were never too far from the silhouettes of that nut-bearing giant, *Castanea sativa*.

After our lunch at Caprese Michelangelo on the first day of walking, I saw a peasant farmer ducking into an open barn door after tending his fowl. He greeted us and seemed curious about travelers with backpacks, so I asked him about the chestnut.

"*Castagne*. We start harvesting in a little less than a month."

"Wood or nuts?"

"Nuts, for a sweet flour. Some people call it *farina di marrone*." This term, I supposed, held an aroma of French culinary influence, wafting over the Alps and Apennines from the west.

"Do you harvest them from this forest?" I said, pointing to the patch of woods in front of us.

"From here, all the way up." He nodded his head toward the mix of dark greens, blue-greens, and yellows, somewhat obscured by fog, that extended all the way up to the mountaintop.

"Are the trees there very old?" I wondered aloud.

"Older than I can remember. Some of those trees, they say, are sprouts from trees planted centuries ago."

"The forest—it was planted by man?"

"Yes, of course. The *castagne*, it is one of our major cultivated crops. Look!"

The fog was lifting, as though a veil were rising, finally revealing the wooded face of the mountain above us. The entire mountainside was embellished with the shapes and colors of chestnuts.

I later learned that Italy produces more chestnuts than any country in the world and that I was walking through the heart of the central Italian stronghold for *castagne*. The uplands between Arezzo, Tiburtino Alto, and Caprese Michelangelo form a sanctuary of one of the oldest tree-cropping traditions anywhere. A nut variety selected from the last locality—Michelangelo's birthplace—is the kind most frequently cultivated across eastern Umbria and western Tuscany. Nevertheless, the low frequency of cultivation of all chestnut varieties today can hardly compare with the constancy with which it was found in the country up until half a century ago, when over two million acres remained covered with chestnut canopies. Over lunch not long after the pilgrimage, Florentine scholar Antonio Cacopardo explained some of the complexity of chestnut forestry traditions to me.

"Keep this in mind: for hundreds of years, the chestnut in the Apennines was like wheat for the rural poor. It covered areas so extensive that it dominated the diet of mountain dwellers. It was their staple."

"Do people still rely on it as a mainstay?"

"No, and that's unfortunate." Antonio shook his head. "Modern Italy does not consume even a fifth of the nuts that were harvested historically."

"Is the decline due to the blight that damaged the trees several decades ago?" I wondered.

"The blight obviously had some effect, but the sad thing is that there was also a demise in traditional agroforestry skills that went hand in hand with the decline in the use of the chestnut as a food. Today, most of the chestnut stands are coming up in secondary growth [of other species], or else they are intensively coppiced for just one product. Before, they maintained chestnut stands of several different ages, each in its own way, to obtain different products."

Some three hundred chestnut products, I learned, ranged from the nuts themselves to tomato stakes, crossties, and fence posts through furniture and boat-building materials. Tannins were extracted from the bark and heartwood to cure heavy leathers. Shingles, panels, and musical instruments could be shaped out of larger logs run through planing mills. Antonio recited this litany of uses, sipped his drink, then continued:

"The two main ways of managing chestnut trees in the past were simply called *macchia* and *selva*. In *macchia*, chestnut trees are kept short and coppiced for poles over a twelve-to-fifteen-year rotation. In *selva*, trees many decades old are tended for the nut harvest and selectively cut for furniture wood and long boards."

A few farming families tenaciously maintain the vestiges of this rotational scheme, a scheme that may take over a century to run its cycle. In Tuscany, one farmer we met was still very selective about which old trees he cuts from the *selva*. And in the gap opened by his harvest, he always plants more trees. Nonetheless, forestry for foodstuffs is now the exception rather than the rule in Italy, where more than half the remaining acreage is frequently coppiced for wood alone. The chestnut blight brought about a collapse in nut production, and by the time the trees had begun to recover, Italian tastes had shifted away from the *castagne* they had formerly adored.

The chestnut blight did not reach southern Europe as early as it did the United States, and the consequences were somewhat different in the Mediterranean than they were along the eastern seaboard. In the United States, the blight fungus may have been introduced with Japanese chestnut imports as early as the 1880s, but soon after killing all the old trees along the avenues of the Bronx Zoo, in New York, it moved rapidly to devastate wild forest and planted grove alike. In less than three decades, the fungus wiped out the equivalent of nine million acres of chestnuts within the eastern deciduous forests.

It became one of the world's greatest forest tragedies. As chestnut ecologist Sandra Anagnostakis wrote in its wake, "We lost a beautiful shade tree, tasty nuts, and exceptional lumber; wildlife lost its most dependable mast producer. . . . Sweeping away every mature American chestnut tree, the infamous blight cut through the New England hardwood forest like an evil plague." Though most wild trees are quite heterogeneous in their susceptibility to diseases, no American chestnut populations had ever been exposed to such a fungus, so virtually no genetic resistance had evolved. From Maine to Georgia, all attempts to protect native stands chemically or physically failed miserably.

Like the blight in the United States, the blight in southern Europe began with the inadvertent introduction of fungus-infected trees from Asia. Some say that around 1939, the blight began to spread around the Mediterranean from diseased nursery stock that had been transplanted into a northern Italian botanical garden; no one really knows its point of origin for sure. As in the United States, the fungus was dispersed both by sticky masses of spores that hitchhiked along with birds, insects, and small mammals and by another, dustlike spore mass carried by the wind. After the fungus entered a wound in the bark of a chestnut tree, it would grow to produce a canker that girdled the trunk. The old trunk usually died, but the base of the tree survived to produce new sprouts at the ground level. The tallest trees that I saw around Caprese Michelangelo were probably the first or second generation of sprouts that had emerged, then survived, following the first wave of dieback.

An oddity had occurred in Italy quite unlike anything noticed in America while the blight took its toll. In 1950, twelve years after the blight's appearance near Genoa, pathology professor Antonio Biraghi observed what he thought were resistant tree sprouts in the area of earliest infection. Even though the trees had been girdled, their cankers were healing, and the shoots rising from them expressed normal vegetative growth. Soon healing cankers and healthy growth were recognized in other areas of Italy as well, but only in areas where the disease had swept through twelve to fifteen years earlier.

As time passed, population after population was seen to recover. This puzzled Biraghi's colleagues, because true genetic resistance could not "spread" from one vegetative sucker to the next, nor could the blight fungus genetically lose its virulence overnight. Finally, Jene Grente, a French expert on fungi, found that there was something parasitizing the blight fungus in northern Italy. When he passed samples on to Sandra Anagnostakis working in New England, she found that Italian blight fungi were suffering from a viruslike infection. She got permission from the government and in-oculated the blight fungus that was infesting the bark of American chestnuts. Once the Italian strains were inoculated on American trees in a greenhouse, Anagnostakis demon-strated that expansion of the cankers was halted so that the trees could survive.

Throughout Italy, the viruslike infection spread on its own, and healing cankers formed as the fungus was nipped in the bud. The fungal disease could no longer penetrate as deeply into the bark, and the trees were able to produce healthy new wood. Forty years after the discovery of the blight in Italy, the disease ceased to be a major problem.

"Forty years!" I moaned to myself the first time I heard this story, stretching my soul up into the bark of the fungus-infected chestnut. "Will it take me forty years to overcome my sores? How long it takes us poor mortals to heal!"

By the time the chestnut groves began to recover, how-ever, chestnut farmers had lost over 80 percent of their

customary consumers. The only market remaining for chestnut flour—and it was rather small—was for pastry making.
Antonio Cacopardo lamented this withering of a staple into
a specialty, but he understood the economics at work: "Even
today, chestnut flour is three times as expensive as wheat
flour. It is used primarily for sweet pastries and confections.
Farina di marrone has one disadvantage in the market today;
for most modern consumers, it seems too sweet to eat in a
meal with meat and vegetables or with beer. Unless you are
accustomed to it, the farina tastes a bit too rich, too strong.

"But in the old days, they would make a fire, heat flat
sandstone slabs, and put a chestnut leaf on top of each one
after it became hot." Antonio put his hand palm up over his
other hand, mimicking the placing of leaf on stone. "Then
they would pour a liquid batter made from chestnut flour
over the leaf, which would keep the batter from sticking to
the stone. The result was an unleavened bread—a tortilla,
really, like those you eat in Mexico. Yes, more like a thick
tortilla, not bread in the typical sense."

"It sounds delicious," I sighed.

"Ah, but there is a problem with such foods nowadays.
The trouble is, no matter how tasty and nutritious this *torta
di castagne* is, the country people today are self-conscious
about it. Eating chestnuts is a sign of poverty. Because wheat
bread is eaten in the city, chestnut bread is associated with
the poor country table. It is the same everywhere with native
crops, no?"

I had been curious about the chestnut's taste and texture
and about whether any country folk still used it for foods

other than desserts. I also wanted to taste it myself. After Ginger and I arrived at Caprese, I took a side trip to the mountaintop village of Fagiollo, where I asked a woman working in her yard about the local availability of chestnut products.

"Would anyone have quantities of chestnut flour stored away? Is it common here?"

"Common? It's our life."

"Do many men here work the chestnut harvest?"

"Men? Do you mean grown men?" She mocked the walk of a stocky man swaggering. "It's not just men, it's all of us. We've been working the chestnuts since we were *bambini*!"

"Well, then, where can I buy some chestnut flour?"

"Try the store up in town that has a sign for the local forest co-op."

The store was filled with local elders. Ginger stayed outside. I walked in, sticking out like a sore thumb.

"Farina di castagne?" The people in the store looked up at me, embarrassed by my question. The store owner read their body language, then politely replied, "Better to come back in three weeks, in November. The harvest hasn't happened yet!"

"Yes, I think I understand. But I won't be here then. I'm not from around here . . ." but as I tried to explain my situation, the old women in the store flashed me looks that emphatically stated that they already knew I was alien to their world. "I'll be far away by harvest time and unable to return for flour. Is there any left from last year's harvest?"

The locals looked up at the storekeeper for his response, then fidgeted with the goods on the shelves. He gave them an icy gaze, then turned back to me.

"I'm sorry, it's just not *fresh*. All we have left is old flour that has sat on the shelves for two or three months. These people think it loses its taste. Around here, I can't even give it away."

The shopkeeper's father overheard the conversation from the next room and came in, smiling, thinking over the situation.

"If this young stranger wants some, let's give him some. He apparently doesn't know the difference. Try to find him a tightly sealed package in the back room. Make sure it's not stale. And give him some kind of discount, for God's sake. He doesn't seem to be a pastry maker, or he would know that he would need a fresh batch."

"Is that all it's used for? Just pastries?"

"No, no. You can make polenta, too."

"But do *you* make polenta—is it often made here?"

"Yes, here we do. Not everywhere, but here, yes."

I knew from my friends Beth and John Romer that chestnuts remain sporadically and seasonally used just to the south of us, on the border between Tuscany and Umbria closer to Lake Cortona. Ginger and I visited them there later. Just as John was pointing out to me the areas in their valley where their neighbor Orlando Cerotti still manages chestnuts on a long rotation, Orlando's wife, Silvana, walked down the lane carrying a basket filled to the brim with freshly picked foods. Silvana had been out harvesting enough green beans and lettuce to fill the basket, but on her way back from the garden, she had tucked wild amaranth greens and mint into her upturned apron. She looked like a walking greengrocer, comfortably moving down the lane in a rayon dress printed with flowers.

Silvana had learned to make sweet chestnut cakes from her mother, and she still makes them as her mother did a half-century ago. Beth Romer described Silvana's process of preparing *baldino di castagna* in the following way:

> The cake is made by mixing the soft sweet flour into a loose paste with water and some warm olive oil. When the paste is well mixed, Silvana pours it into a round flat tin which has been oiled, again with olive oil. Sometimes Silvana flavors the cake by scattering rosemary over the top and sometimes a little lemon peel cut into tiny splinters. To cook it she puts the flat tin on top of some embers beside the fire, then covers it with an old saucepan lid, on top of which she piles more hot embers. In this way she has constructed a primitive oven. This is how the cake was cooked when she was a girl, though now she very often puts it into her new oven on medium heat. The cake is done when the top has become a dark chestnut brown and has a cracked surface. There is also a delicious smell of nuts and chocolate. . . . The olive oil and the rosemary, so often the garnish for meats, impart a curious . . . old-fashioned taste.

As for the simpler, unleavened cake called *castagnaccia*, which once served as daily bread for many Tuscans, it has largely fallen out of use, Silvana and the Romers agreed. The reason? "It is a poor food that still brings back memories of deprivation."

The Cerottis and many of their neighbors continue to care deeply about what goes into their mouths and where those foods come from. Quite often, their other foods, like chestnuts, still come from the managed forests immediately around them. For that reason, it is a misnomer to call all this forest bounty a *wild harvest*; many of the trees that have been harvested were earlier planted, or pruned, or protected from competitors. Nevertheless, the hill people of Italy still consume many times the amount of forest products that the average American does—in fact, more than most forest-dwelling Native Americans do today.

As Ginger and I walked down into the Tiber valley after our visit with the chestnuts and the Cerottis, she marveled at the beauty and the fine ecological tuning she sensed in their highly managed valley. "It's not wilderness, but it *is* a cultured landscape peopled at an appropriate scale," Ginger mused. I nodded in agreement, but glanced around, looking to see if it retained enough wildness to suit me. "Harmony!" Ginger added, slowing her walk as she noticed my intense interest in this landscape. "You're talking about people living in *harmony* with their surroundings, just as I've seen on the Hopi mesas or in the mountains of Nepal."

"Harmony, huh?" I said, chuckling.

"What are you grinning about, Gary?"

"Do you know what they called you back in the hotel in Florence, Ms. Harmon? *Signora Harmony*. The desk clerk kept referring to you as *Signora Harmony*! I think I'll call you *Sister* Harmony the rest of the trip. It fits you, and, yes, it fits this land."

As our shadows grew longer, bumping against one another, then merging with the coming darkness, Ginger and I walked on toward Anghiari. Long after the sun went down, we finally entered that hilltop town on the edge of the Tiber valley and began our search for an inn where we could gain some well-deserved rest.

Interlude 3
The Night of the Fight

e had continued our walk, without incident, from Caprese, down onto the edge of the Tiber valley at Anghiari by nightfall. Whatever we dined on that night in Anghiari was not memorable; at least, it could not top the gnocchi and *porcini* mushrooms we had eaten in Caprese at midday. What *was* memorable about Anghiari was the street fighting. I am not talking about drive-by murders or gang wars with switchblades. I am talking about verbal battles that erupted from teases and testy challenges into a cacophony of shouting, jeering, roaring, and soaring insults. Because I was in bed, behind closed curtains when it began, I could not tell how many men were involved—perhaps at first three or four, commenting on another man passing by who was talking with a woman they knew. After his first counterattack on them, I did not hear a woman's voice again, but more and more men joined the mob, taking one side or the other. After the first outburst of screaming and high-pitched heckling, I dashed to the window and looked down on the street, worried that someone had been bloodied.

I was wrong. Several men had gathered as a shield around one man, and others were calming three other men down, but everyone was still standing, unscathed. Several older men made moral proclamations and moved from one side to the other, appealing with gestures and heartfelt words to the younger men in each pack. Under the weight of these appeals, a few of the younger men defected, simply walking away from the scene, making their own impassioned proclamations as they went. After twenty minutes, the entire mob dispersed into bars and down alleys, all of them continuing to talk heatedly to their comrades, all offering at once their own interpretations of what had really happened.

If that much testosterone had been let loose in one place in Los Angeles or South Phoenix, a dozen brothers would have died from gunshot or knife wounds. However frightening or unpleasant to hear, the fighting had been neither toxic nor fatal. I was amazed.

I was suddenly reminded of the tensions, eruptions, and distress that had led to my divorce. Married to a woman whom I still consider one of the gentlest and most peaceful people I have ever met, I had watched our partnership erode into discord, with heated arguments that later made sense to neither of us.

"You can't hear each other anymore," a therapist declared. "Your relationship has become toxic. It is poisoning both of you and distorting your reactions to each other. Do you understand? You have become ruinous to each other's lives!"

I was also reminded of the famous study that made all the papers when I was in college: co-eds who shared a dormitory kept track of their menstrual cycles all the while they lived together. As certain groups of these women became closer friends, the start of their periods would converge on the same dates. Does a similar phenomenon happen among men who frequent the same bar every fortnight to watch a soccer game, yelling and drinking and carrying on? Do their testosterone levels all go over the brink together at the same time, on hot summer nights when a favorite team has let them down?

And what happens to men and women, husbands and wives, when their mood swings either synchronize or, for some other reason, radically diverge? How much effect do they have on each other's periodicities, high tides, and ebbs?

The street fighting had stopped by eleven, but I was still awake when the village bells rang at midnight. I got up again and went to the window to look for the moon. From my vantage point, I could not see its light, but I wanted to know of its pull on me. I paused by the window for a minute longer, but my fatigue led me back to bed. I soon fell asleep without any moonbeams having entered my room.

At the end of our journey, when the full moon rose over Monte Subasio on the Feast of Saint Francis in Assisi, I remembered the lunar leanness of that time in Anghiari. The moon, like the flower of the *panporcino* that I could find only on sacred mountains, became a sign: its presence or absence mirrored how full or how empty a place—and a moment —felt to me.

Chapter 4

*Corn has got to grow on these little shelves of earth . . . and if
the terraces are too narrow to plough, the peasant digging them
will still leave the grassy lip, because it helps to hold the surface
in the rains. And here the flowers take refuge. Over and over and
over and over has the soil been turned, twice a year, sometimes
three times a year, for several thousands of years. Yet the flowers
have never been driven out. . . . In England, in America, the
flowers get rooted out, driven back. They become fugitive. But in
the intensive cultivation of ancient Italian terraces, they dance
round and hold their own.*

D. H. LAWRENCE

*In the valley . . . wherever [maize] was grown, it was inevitably
the poor . . . who had to take without enthusiasm to eating
cornmeal cakes instead of bread. . . . The peasant ate maize and
sold his wheat.*

FERNAND BRAUDEL

Sagra di Polenta: Bitter Herbs and the Bread of Poverty

I could not believe my eyes when Ginger and I first dipped down into the Etruscan valleys. They were thick with summer crops laid out in long rows, the same crops that I had seen in most Native American farming villages from the Rio Grande pueblos of New Mexico through the Mayan highlands of Guatemala. There they were, my old neighbors: maize, tobacco, and sunflowers in the fields; beans, amaranths, and squash in the gardens. As we walked along the weedy edges of field after field filled with thousands of transplants from the New World, I felt like I had arrived at a family reunion, a house filled with relatives, some of whom I loved and some whom I accepted or tolerated only because they were my kin.

Here, a third of the way around the world from my birthplace, I had not expected to be overwhelmed by such familiars as I had grown up with in Indiana and have grown myself in Arizona. I could feel the same sweltering heat rising from the crop canopies, and I shielded my eyes from the same insipid greens that glanced sunlight back into the broad sky. Throughout the day following our night in Anghiari, as we walked to Città di Castello, we never lost sight of fields of American crops and flowering weeds. We walked ten miles on the edges of fields and hedgerows, the likes of which we would have avoided like the plague if we had been going for a hike back home.

It was then that I remembered those words of Saint Francis that had originally propelled me on this path: "All which you used to avoid will bring you great sweetness and exceeding joy." I had once avoided cultured, hybridized landscapes, seeking the wild and the native only in their purest forms. Here, I was not likely to find native Europe, no more than native America, but I might encounter something altogether beyond my expectations. Here was the paradox that Lawrence described so well: "It is queer that a country so perfectly cultivated as Tuscany, where half the produce of five acres of land will have to support ten human mouths, still has so much room for the wildflowers and the nightingale."

We would follow whatever tracks we found running through these soils, no matter how long they had been worked. I could not have guessed that beneath the neat, glossy sheen of modern hybrid crops, I would notice the distended underbelly of peasant culture, a culture that barely survived on rustic breads laced with hallucinatory herbs. Until I saw the hunger and disease that shaped the hopes and dreams of the historic Italian peasants, I had no sense of the compost out of which Saint Francis had sprouted seven centuries ago.

We dropped from the balconies of *macchia* scrubland down to the valley floor where every inch of soil seemed to have been under the machine-drawn plow. These are among the longest-cultivated bottomlands in all of Italy and perhaps among the least diverse in crop production. Once we left the hilltop village of Anghiari, I was struck by the sudden ballooning of the size of fields: hundreds of acres sat filled with a single crop, burgeoning with either drying sunflowers, hybrid maize, rank tobacco, or uniform stands of soybeans.

Ginger likened them to American suburbs in the fifties, devoid of any expression of ethnic diversity: "They're single-class communities, those suburbs, these fields, just like tree plantations. Hardly anything grows under them, no birds sing in their midst."

We made it a game, walking the miles of dirt roads out of Anghiari, to look for anything that disrupted the order, any plant that emerged from below the engineered crop canopy. I delighted in finding parasitic broomrapes ravaging the roots of sunflowers. Ginger noticed vestigial hedges along field and ditch edges. I tallied up their inhabitants: hops, sprawling rosebushes, nettles, locusts, and feral apples.

Finches erupted out of the thorny mass of one hedgerow; hooded crows cawed and cackled above us as we crossed the Tiber floodplain and approached Città di Castello. We failed to notice such birds and weeds only in the manicured tobacco fields that were swarming with poor farmworkers, stomping down the aisles, stooping to cut the rank growth by hand, and stashing the odorous leaves on portable drying racks. There, the human presence overwhelmed us, and our eyes were not fixed on the ground.

By the time we limped into sight of the stone walls of Città di Castello, I felt awed by the tenacity of the weedy herbs that stain and flavor everything in the Italian countryside. There were amaranths and grasses rooted in the sheerest of stone walls and doves wherever a space was found large enough for a nest. Even along the roadside—regardless of how narrow, how frequently mowed, how incessantly sprayed—the flowering herbs were indomitable: filaree and gypsywort; comfrey, chicory, and timothy; butter-and-eggs, cheeseweed; hawkbit and foxtail; sow thistle, lamb's-quarters, and hogweed; mustards, false basils, borages, and sages. When I took off my socks and jeans that evening in a small room above a café, I found barbed and bristly seeds, sticky leaves, and stains of golden pollen coating my clothes from my calves to my ankles.

In 1648, Ovidio Montalbani explained that such weeds were not at all peripheral to Mediterranean culture but had been and would continue to be essential to human welfare: "Hundreds and hundreds of different roots, buds, fruits, and seeds of herbs are edible and can well pass into the diet with little artifice." Between 1600 and 1650, when Italy's population dropped by almost two million due to the plague, the distribution of food supplies was periodically disrupted by regional epidemics; to get by, survivors found themselves turning to foraging beyond their fields and gardens. To help the unacquainted, many of them on the verge of starvation, Montalbani offered instructions on how to gain sufficient sustenance from the wild herbs in the rural landscape.

It turned out that many people soon needed to heed his words. Suddenly, price controls on grains triggered a collapse in the bread market, and increasingly oppressive sharecropping policies kept peasants from having either the buying power or the land to grow much food to feed themselves. The poor had been left poorer, forced to give the bulk of their cultivated produce to their landlords and to glean whatever nutrients they could from the spontaneous vegetation left around them. They began to live outside the formal economy; in much the same manner, Francis and his followers had survived in the woods and swamps four centuries before.

Then, in the hundred years following 1650, Italy's population grew by four million, and there were nearly 50 percent more mouths to feed off the same amount of land than there had been in 1492. By the 1740s, cold snaps and other climatic fluctuations had reduced the quantity and variety of food crops being produced in Italy, and agricultural yields could no longer keep up with population growth. Hungry peasants again turned to wild greens and starchy roots as mainstays during the warmer seasons. During the winter, they were forced to rely on rustic breads made from stale or larvae-ridden flours and meals.

To extend their grains as far as the resource could go, they added to the batter herbs or their seeds, some of them bitter, mildly toxic, or potently psychotropic. Folk historian

Piero Camporesi explains this survival strategy in *Bread of Dreams*: "Through operations of simple magic, the camouflaging and metamorphosis of flavors, the denaturing and recycling of herbs—even the most unpleasant—provided for the neutralizing of poisonous herbs and . . . [rendered] pleasing the taste of those which were repulsive. The artifice derived from 'natural magic' would extend bread miraculously: a saving demon for a starving populace."

It was a "saving demon" because the hunger was masked more than it was quelled; the poor remained exploited and undernourished, but the narcotic herbs buffered them from this reality. This dark tradition of escaping from hunger through drug-laden meals is what has come down to us in the diluted forms of dill-laced loaves of rye bread and of poppyseed cake. But the narcotic white poppy seeds sown for centuries amid the fava bean fields of Tuscany were not the only psychoactive seed kneaded into the dough. Among the poor, *poppyseed bread* came to mean any bread "disguised and flavored, and in addition spiced with coriander seeds, anise, cumin, sesame-seed oil, and all the possible delectable additives available in the vegetable kingdom, with which man dwelled in a close intimacy, today unthinkable. In areas where it was cultivated," Camporesi adds, "even the flour of hemp seeds was used in the kitchen to prepare doughs and breads which 'cause the loss of reason' and 'generate domestic drunkenness and a certain stupidity.' "

It is no shock that such plants were used by the peasantry; what is startling is that Camporesi believes that for several centuries, many of the poor of southern Europe were immersed in general states of domestic drunkenness and delirium, conditions induced "with the help of hallucinogenic seeds and herbs, arising from the background of chronic malnourishment and hunger . . . the simplest and most natural producer of mental alterations and dreamlike states."

Knowledge about such mind-altering herbs was no doubt ancient in southern Europe, but dependence on them probably resurfaced whenever social or environmental stresses ravaged the poor. If Saint Francis did indeed live and eat as the poor of his times lived and ate, he was inevitably exposed to these herbs and influenced by their qualities. Camporesi does not let this possibility slip by unnoticed; instead, he suggests that Saint Francis was, in all likelihood, an "eccentric wizard of ecstasy in a body consumed by penance and privation, his mind altered by fasts, like certain hermits kept alive by roots and herbs [that] stimulated the same sense of the real and the impossible as experienced by those who, suffering and subdued by an involuntary poverty . . . fell into shocking hallucinations and stupefied contemplations."

Perhaps Francis himself was a voluntary victim of hunger and herbal hallucination, for we know that he suffered as well from the oozing wounds of leprosy, the incessant pain of arthritis, and four dozen other maladies and degenerative diseases by the time he died.

It may sound like blasphemy for Camporesi to attribute the "vision" and "saintly wounds" of Francis to the same dream-inducing diets and diseases that the poor of his times experienced, but young Bernardone set out to experience fully the "immeasurable treasure of most holy poverty" that he had not experienced while growing up in a privileged family. His meditative powers may have moved him into sublime trancelike states at times, but spoiled breads and narcotic herbs may have enhanced Francis's reputed capacities to talk with animals, to endure unspeakable pain, and to survive freezing nights or red-hot coals. We retell the stories of when he soared like a hero but forget the many times he suffered the same insults that any poor European must have suffered. Father Roy Gasnick has quipped, "Americans gravitate not to Francis the sufferer but to Francis standing in the birdbath," despite the fact that during the last six years of his life, the saint could hardly stand as upright as his statues now portray him.

As Italians multiplied and their population recovered after the plague, there was only one thing that staved off hunger and herbal hallucinations for the bulk of them: maize. Word of this productive summer crop from the Americas may have arrived in Italy as early as 1494, via letters from Guglielmo Coma, who accompanied Columbus on his second voyage. A pamphlet written in Latin and published in Pavia in December of that year told of "a prolific kind of grain, the size of a lupin, rounded like a chick-pea. When broken, it produces a fine flour, and it is ground like wheat. A bread of excellent flavor is made from it." The pamphleteer, Nicolò Syllacio, added a comment that tells less about corn's presumed use in the Americas and more about how it would be consumed in times of stress in Europe. Speaking from fourth-hand knowledge of Native American farmers, Syllacio claimed that "many who have little food simply chew the grains without preparation."

Some European historians claim that maize had arrived in Florence and was being grown in botanical gardens there within ten years of Syllacio's pamphlet being distributed.

What strikes me is that by the 1530s and 1540s, it had spread beyond the botanical elite of Europe and was being grown by the masses, many of whom assumed that it had been brought from Asia Minor. Like many items introduced from foreign lands through Islamic traders, it was attributed to the "Turks," or Moors, and was commonly called *frumentum turcicum* or *granoturco*. Of its true origin, Italian herbalist Petrus Matthiolus knew better, and said so in 1565: "This type of grain, which they wrongly called *turcicum*, can be numbered among the varieties of wheat. [They have named it] incorrectly I say, because it ought to be called *indicum* not *turcicum*, for it was brought from the West Indies, not out of Turkey and Asia."

By the time Matthiolus wrote these words, maize had already come into widespread cultivation among the peasants in the Venetian states, Lombardy, and north central Italy. Within another three or four decades, *granoturco* had even begun to appear prominently in economic production summaries for northern Italy. Because it could be planted in the warm season after the harvest of wheat, barley, and buckwheat, it complemented rather than competed with the traditional winter cereals, allowing farmers to double-crop the same piece of land and to produce grain year round. By the end of the eighteenth century, maize had eclipsed wheat and other winter grains in total yields in many of the northern and central Italian provinces.

When it came to keeping the poor fed, maize, it appeared, would make all the difference in the world. Arthur Young, an English traveler to the Mediterranean, summarized the situation in the 1780s: "Where there is no maize, there are fallows; and where there are fallows, the people starve for

want. For the inhabitants of a country to live upon that
[maize] plant, which [prepares the ground] for wheat and at
the same time keeps their cattle fat . . . is to possess a
treasure."

It may come as no surprise that such a treasure would
inspire the Italian populace to glorify and praise their adopted
miracle crop. One such cultural celebration of maize is the
Sagra di Polenta, a festival still celebrated near the border
between Tuscany and Umbria. Ginger and I decided to stay
over an extra day in the Valtiberina Alta near Città di Castello
so that we could participate in this pageant in honor of
cornmeal mush.

After accepting a ride from Città di Castello to Monterchi,
we walked across a bridge and through corn-adorned gates
at the base of the hilltop village. As I looked at the ears and
stalks decorating the arc across the road, it dawned on me
that hybrid dent corn from the midwestern United States
was the icon of the day. I was perplexed, I guess, because I
had read somewhere of at least eight heirloom varieties of
maize in Italy, ranging from white and red late-maturing
races to beaked and dwarfed early varieties. After several
hundred years of maize cultivation near Monterchi, the farmers should have accumulated their own races that would be
favored over recently introduced midwestern dents. Ginger
patiently waited while I asked elderly Monterchi residents if
they had favorite kinds of corn that they grew here year after
year.

"Oh, certainly, I can show you," one man said to me
enthusiastically. He then pleaded with me to stay put so that
he could bring me evidence of the range of maize they grew
on the bottomland surrounding the town. He returned a few

minutes later with a stack of brochures from multinational hybrid maize breeding firms.

"Look at all the kinds of *granoturco* that are accessible to us! We don't grow all of them in this area each year, but I've tried some from nearly every one of these companies!"

I read aloud the company names and the hymns of praise by their agronomists who had put the hybrids through last year's variety trials. In slick, color-printed handbills, Italian farmers were offered a cadre of seven hybrids from DeKalb; fifteen from Asgrow; eighteen from Pioneer Hybrid; and finally, fourteen dents from Agrigenetics, including new releases named Las Vegas and Dragon, for those farmers who loved gambling and fantasy.

The maize varieties were recent immigrants, but there was nevertheless something profoundly traditional about this folk festival. The *sagra* pays homage to a food of the poor and celebrates polenta in all its forms: grilled, baked, or fried, glorified by spices, embellished by savory sauces, served side by side with sausage, truffles, or calf livers, swallowed down with local wines or with draft beers.

While Ginger wandered the streets, I went to watch and talk with six white-haired men in equally white smocks and chef's hats, decorated with husklike green bandannas; all of them were slightly drunk. Between slapstick routines that recounted their shared exploits, these polenta pros were dumping cornmeal into twenty-gallon cauldrons, where it was being mechanically blended with boiling water at the bottom and churned with wooden spoons by hand at the top. The batter of one part cornmeal to three parts water belched and blistered over a small wood fire.

Every twenty minutes, three of the old men would pick

up the cauldron to ladle the steaming mush out into a wooden box six feet long by three feet wide and four inches deep. Using their huge wooden spoons, the polenta chefs spread the mush flat like an enormous cake of butter, smoothing its surface, then letting it cool. Once the haze of steam had cleared its surface, it had lost enough heat to allow the chefs to work with it, simply scooping heaps into bowls for waiting customers or preparing more elaborate dishes for later sale. According to the customer's request, a vendor might add a sauce of fresh and pureed tomatoes, olive oil, carrots, onion, sausage, garlic, or dill seed, or sprinkle on Parmesan cheese. Other cooks let the corn cakes harden longer so that they could be cut into squares and grilled next to juicy sausages and livers, whose grease sprayed and saturated the corn with their taste.

Once Ginger and I rejoined to talk with the old men, they handed us bowl after bowl of the polenta, soon forgetting to charge us, then refusing our offerings of lire. They began to ask us as many questions as we asked them. While we leaned against wreaths of wild sunflowers and dried ears of dent corn, Ginger nudged me and whispered, "Ask these local farmers, and I'll bet they'll tell you that corn is a native here."

I did, and they did. They pushed forward one of the oldest, most drunken cooks, who took another sip of his beer before offering me their official testimony on the corn's antiquity.

"Maize has been here always, as long as we as a people have been here. It is what has always fed our village," he said, turning for confirmation to his cronies. They solemnly agreed, but one of their sons winked at me. Later, this son leaned over the counter and offered another perspective.

"My father does not know world history as I do, but maize has only been grown here since it was brought from Native Americans. Of course, some of us know that its Indian name is maize, not *granoturco* like most of them call it here."

The elders were innocent of any understanding of American Indian contributions to their crop. Nevertheless, I sensed that many of my Native American friends would have felt at home with the festival itself. It had many of the components of traditional celebrations found anywhere in the world: the crowning of a queen; a race between the men; a social dance; plant decorations in praise and thanks for an abundant harvest; plenty of rich food and hearty drink. And it seemed to me that corn, among all crops, was particularly likely to become laden with cultural expressions wherever it traveled from its Neotropical birthplace—expressions that were remarkably similar to those of the Mesoamerican cultures that had first nurtured it. I simply cannot imagine the Italians, Mayans, Tarahumara, or Hidatsa making a comparable fuss over alfalfa, soybeans, or rapeseed.

Whatever cultural elaborations Italians had independently evolved in their nurturing of corn, they did not, until this century, rediscover one of the essentials of using maize as a staple: processing it with ash, calcium bicarbonate "lime," or other mineral salts as a means of releasing its essential nutrients in forms that would be available to the human metabolism.

This oversight had grave consequences, for until maize is processed in such a manner, its niacin remains bound. The amino acid tryptophan cannot be converted to niacin until it is made available by hydrolysis with either lime water or other sodium solutions, which is exactly what Native Americans did in making hominy or ash breads wherever maize was their mainstay. Sadly, Italians received the Mesoamerican maize without knowledge of the native processing techniques that would render it most nutritious. As a result, the regions where Italians were most dependent on maize suffered from an epidemic called pellagra, which is a severe nutritional deficiency rather than an infectious disease. This affliction further crazed the poor and hungry, pushing them over the brink into delusions and hallucinations far worse than those that the spoiled, herb-laden breads of previous centuries had given them.

Pellagra as an affliction was described relatively recently and appears to have been entirely absent in American lands where corn was native. But by 1730, a Spanish physician, Gaspar Casal, was noticing an undescribed mania and delirium setting in among the corn-eating poor of his country. He noted that the common folk called this affliction *mal de la rosa*, for the reddish spots and horrible scabby crusts that appeared on the skin of those who later lost their minds. By 1740, the same disease had been described by Italian physicians, who called it *pelle agra*, or "sour skin." A 1771 treatise by Dr. Francisco Frapoli described how truly terrible pellagra becomes:

> *The disease rages recurrently until at length the skin no longer peels, but becomes wrinkled, thickened, and full of fissures. Then, for the first time, the patient begins to have trouble in the head: fear, sadness, wakefulness and vertigo, mental stupor bordering on*

fatuity, hypochondria, fluxes from the bowels, and sometimes,
mania. Then the strength of the body fails . . . [and the patient
becomes] most resistant to all remedies, consumed with a ghastly
wasting, [until it reaches] the last extremes.

By 1784, 5 percent of the population of certain Italian
provinces suffered from the malady, and 20 percent of the
inhabitants in some hill-country farm towns were debilitated.
Tuscany was fifth in the severity of the pellagra epidemic
among the Italian provinces, while Umbria was third. In
Tuscany maize had become the major agricultural product
on 65,000 acres of land, and it was clear that the farmworkers
who ate polenta as their mainstay were the most susceptible.
The malady became so widespread that the first large insane
asylum was established in Milan in 1784 to serve as a *pel-
lagrosario*, and even a quarter of a century later, nearly two-
thirds of those confined in this hospital were deranged by
pellagra. Asylums were soon established in other regions as
well, but all pellagra sufferers could not be so contained;
many remained on the land. When Goethe crossed into Italy
from the north in 1786, he not only found the disease com-
monplace but related its presence to the consumption of
polenta:

I noticed as soon as it was daylight a definite change in their
[northern Italians'] physical appearance. I thought the sallow
complexion of the women particularly disagreeable. Their features
spoke of misery and their children looked as pitiful. The men
looked little better. . . . I believe that their unhealthy condition
is due to their constant diet of maize and buckwheat, or as they
call them, yellow polenta and black polenta.

These are ground fine, the flour is boiled in water to a thick mush and then eaten. In the German Tirol they separate the dough into small pieces and fry them in butter, but in the Italian Tirol the polenta is eaten just as it is or sometimes with a sprinkling of grated cheese. Meat they never see from one year's end to the other.

Despite such early intuitions that pellagra was due to a lack of dietary variety, it wasn't until 1905 that the key factors were clarified. At first, social reformers gained some success in reducing pellagra by increasing the food choices available to the poor, even when poverty itself could not be eliminated. Clinicians, on the other hand, chose to provide vitamin supplements of niacin in order to reduce the dominance of leucine over tryptophan in the amino acid balance of the overall diet. European health workers ignored an equally effective solution first proposed by a Mexican physician, Ismael Salas, while lecturing in Europe in 1863; he wanted to teach the peasants to eat corn as lime-soaked tortillas instead of as polenta—in other words, to introduce to Europeans the niacin-releasing food preparation method of Mesoamericans that had not arrived with the maize itself centuries before.

Nevertheless, Italy lagged behind Spain and France in controlling pellagra. Some historians claim that this is because the Italian government was not as effective in changing the food habits of its polenta eaters, but more likely, it was unwilling to tackle the causes of poverty and oppression that kept many peasants on the verge of starvation. Instead, it launched huge sanitation campaigns to keep corn from being spoiled by "pellagra-causing microbes." Worse yet, some public health workers claimed that pellagra was hereditary, so that the poor could not be helped.

Elsewhere, other health workers treated the disease as if it were infectious, a fear that generated racism against Italians in the United States. A U.S. commission on pellagra reported that an American woman died in 1894 after contracting the disease from immigrant Italian farmworkers. In American cities, a common turn-of-the-century rumor took another twist: immigrants had carried with them from Italy foods contaminated with a pellagra-causing fungus. Perhaps mycophobic Anglo-Americans thought that Italians were so recklessly indulgent with edible fungi that they would let the fungi spread.

By 1930, pellagra victims could be found in only a few Italian hospitals, and the Italian sanitation programs to eradicate it had been dismantled. When Daphne Roe visited Italian hospitals in the 1950s—half a century after a 1904 Italian commission enacted a law to eliminate pellagra permanently—he found that "it had virtually disappeared from northern Italy. I was not innocent enough to believe that this change was due to a law. Rather, the *mezzadria* [sharecropper] system had died out, the tenant farmer had gained independence, and the poor could for the most part 'inherit the earth.'"

Nevertheless, there was something in Roe and the Italian physicians she visited that still blamed the peasants for the persistence of the disease, as if their allegiance to "primitive" food traditions had kept them from being helped earlier by scientists. Dr. Ferdinando Serri could show Roe only one "prematurely old woman, clothed in old-fashioned black garments, who bore the classic traits of the disease on her skin.

. . . Here was a [sole] case to show foreign visitors; I was having a demonstration of a condition which persisted only among the people of the backwoods, who through a combination of ignorance and poverty continued to follow their traditional food customs."

Ignorance, poverty, and traditional foods—if we are to dismiss all food customs of the poor and uneducated as being maladaptive and based on ignorance, then we have to account in some other way for the absence of pellagra during thousands of years of traditional maize processing in the Americas. It is easy to dismiss the uneducated as ignorant; on the other hand, it was the educated European elite who failed to bring the secret of maize processing along with the corn seed that they obtained in the Americas. It took educated European doctors two centuries from the time of pellagra's first clinical description to understand the chemical, biological, and social context of niacin deficiency. In the meantime, poor peasants continued to suffer the most as professional health workers tried out one faulty solution after another to quell the epidemic.

At its root, the pellagra problem emerged precisely because educated Europeans disregarded the traditional knowledge of native maize processors. They did not pay sufficient attention to it when they first extracted this miracle crop from its traditional setting; neither did they heed the words of Mexican health worker Ismael Salas when he alerted the European medical profession to the value of the lime-soaked tortilla in preventing pellagra in 1863, seventy years before the disease was finally curbed.

As I looked around at the faces of people, rich and poor, attending the Sagra di Polenta, I could not bring myself to dismiss their affection for polenta as retrograde or ignorant. If they could have gone with Columbus to encounter maize farmers in the Americas, their attention to the details of food processing probably would have allowed them to learn of lime soaking and adding ash to maize. We cannot now turn back the clock, but we can learn to respect surviving ethnic food traditions for the hidden knowledge they may contain. And we can celebrate the gifts—native or other—that have been bestowed on us, learning from the mistakes made in the past that kept us from fully appreciating such gifts.

Bellies full, Ginger and I finally abandoned our places in the polenta-cooking arenas. We gravitated toward the dance floor, where it was plain to see the anomalous mix of custom and modernity that rural Italy embraces.

I watched rows of teenagers, dressed to kill, in outfits ranging from bib overalls and black high-top sneakers to fantasy gowns as bizarre as those in Milan fashion shows. They flirted and looked bored or pained, as hormonally impaired juveniles do anywhere in the world. What pained them the most was when the piped-in rock-and-roll music was turned off so that a polka band could take the stand.

A motley crew of middle-agers brought out accordion, alto sax, bass guitar, and barrelhouse piano. To the teenagers' disgust, the band played a brand of polkas, mazurkas, waltzes, and schottisches that would have been welcome from Lithuania and Romania to the Mexican and Indian villages in my desert homeland. A couple in their eighties took the dance floor; the teenagers glanced away, while everyone else looked on with interest. The arena to themselves, the elderly pair elegantly turned a waltz through its cycles before bowing and inviting other couples to share the floor with them. As the band beat out the tempo of a vigorous polka, younger married couples felt obliged to take up the old-timers on their invitation.

By this time, six kinds of draft beer were coursing through bloodstreams, and the kegs were nearly empty. Tired but upbeat farmworkers appeared, ones who had toiled all day cutting tobacco leaves. They had downed several mugs of beer or glasses of wine as soon as they arrived. Now they were moved by the music and began to find their spouses and in-laws among the tables of peasants congregated off to the side. The dance floor filled as the shadows of the late afternoon descended on the stone walls of Monterchi.

I remembered a man from a nearby village who had told me stories of Sardinian sheepherders coming to these *sagre*, using them as their only release after weeks of twelve-hour workdays. He recalled how one massive Sardinian danced a mazurka without ever letting his dainty partner's feet touch the ground. Others would show their prowess by balancing two wooden chairs on each of their outstretched arms or by stacking up bricks to see who could carry the largest pile.

Ginger and I descended from the village as the last glints of sunlight stained the cornfields below. Our eyes drank up the saturated colors: umber brown soils, terra-cotta roofs, beige and cream stuccoed walls, and yellow splotches of wild sunflowers amid the dark greens of well-fertilized corn.

But these calming tones and textures were juxtaposed with lead-colored antennae, concrete telephone poles, metallic loudspeakers, and electric signs. Ginger and I rode the last bus heading back to the vicinity of our inn in Città di

Castello. We talked about "purity" and how it infects landscape photography, high-brow literature, and gourmet cooking. Why, we wondered, do the purists feel the need to edit out the delightful incongruities, the ironies that wreak havoc on idealized landscapes?

God bless the Sardinian transplant to the Tiber floodplain, dancing in high-topped sneakers to the beat of polkas played on electric accordions hooked to wah-wah pedals. And God bless the New World crop, *granoturco*, which has been in the Valtiberina Alta since the beginning . . . or at least since the Turks brought its *siciliano* seed from Mexico.

And if God can't bless them, then perhaps Saint Francis can, for he is rightfully the patron saint of contradiction and paradox. He inspired grain farmers to leave their fields to become monks, only to tell them later that they could stay and be brothers to the crops. He inspired Columbus to go across the ocean to discover the Garden of Eden, and Columbus brought back to Europe maize seeds to prove he had been there. The Native Americans missionized by the Franciscan friends of Columbus claim that the saint is still wandering among them, out in the desert scrub where they live. He is probably looking for a good bowl of polenta, lime or no lime, and a few pungent herbs to help get him through the night.

Interlude 4
Dancing Through Life

inger and I returned to Città di Castello weary, as if it were the middle of the night. Not so for the local Umbrians, who were still out on *passeggiata*, promenading in the streets, or on the make in clubs and taverns. Their sports cars flashed by us on the larger avenues, while the streets closest to the central plaza were blocked off and mobbed with dancing youth. Rock music wafted through the air like some communal drug.

The dress of the couples on the streets ran the gamut from well-tapered suits and glittery dresses to stone-washed designer jeans, cowboy boots, and T-shirts celebrating Madonna and Black Sabbath.

"Have you ever seen so many gestures, so many animated faces?" Ginger asked me as we edged through a crowd of flirtatious college-age Umbrians.

"I don't have the energy left to take it all in," I muttered. "After a few days of walking, I'm lifeless by eight o'clock in the evening."

Ginger was going to respond, but suddenly the crowd parted to let a police car reach the *piazza centrale*. I watched to see if the young police officers were there to respond to an emergency or to make an announcement. No, they had driven in to catch up on all the social action. Within a minute, each was talking with a group of admiring young women. I rolled my eyes at Ginger, and we headed back to the hotel for a nightcap before hitting the sack.

Two glasses of *grappa* arrived at our small table, and we sipped the flavored brandies in the relative silence and calm of the little hotel.

Ginger finally sighed and said, "That was as good as life gets: that elderly couple out on the dance floor, waltzing with such finesse."

"They must have been in their eighties, but they didn't miss a beat," I agreed.

"After waltzing with each other for decades, it's as though they've *become* the dance!"

I nodded.

"We can all do that, you know," Ginger mused.

"What? Not me? I can do the chicken-scratch—you

know, that down-on-the-ground version of the polka that
my O'odham Indian friends taught me—and I can sometimes
do the Western swing, but waltzes? My feet freeze whenever
they have to count one-two-three, one-two-three, for more
than a minute."

"No, I didn't mean that we can all waltz, Gary. I meant
that we can move through life as if it's a dance. That's the
way O. J. Simpson used to describe running with a football
under his arm. That's the way Royal Robbins and the other
Yosemite climbers used to approach the rock face of Half
Dome—just dance right up it!"

"And what's your dance, madam?" I asked.

"Well, I've had that feeling while canyoneering and on
long-distance treks like this one. I've even found the dance
while cross-country skiing."

"I've felt something when I was doing cross-country, too,
I suppose . . . when the rhythm of the rise and fall of the
earth takes you over?" Ginger let me continue.

"What puzzles me is how I can run the same three-mile
route through the desert four or five times a week, sometimes
daydreaming a little as I go along, but my times are usually
about the same. Then, once in every ten runs along the same
trail, I suddenly kick into overdrive, enjoying every step and
leap. My time is usually a minute and half faster than
the average when that happens. It's as if my consciousness
moves out of my head, to where my feet are touching the
ground . . ."

Ginger smiled at me and took another sip of her *grappa*.
"But I'm not just referring to *sport*, Gary. I mean that we
can approach every adventure in life as a dance."

"Oh, I see what you're getting at. Regardless of our

skills or discipline, we still need that pulse, that rhythm. We need to focus on the moment . . . There is a feeling that comes when I'm fully alert to what's happening around me —what my biology buddies call *the naturalist's trance!*"

"Dance or trance, focused on the moment is right." Ginger chuckled. "Try rock climbing or even driving in rush-hour traffic without being alert! You'll end up with broken bones!" Then she asked me, "Have you ever noticed that quality in anyone else's movements?"

"Another human or another animal? Well, if you've ever seen a wolf or a coyote stalking its prey: ears perked, eyes glued, every hair erect and reading what is in the wind, nose absorbing any scent . . ."

"How about that quality in another person?" Ginger probed.

"Sure, I've seen it when Caroline does her 'ranger-robic' exercises in the evenings." I was referring to our mutual friend, park ranger Caroline Wilson, who had become my hiking companion a few months after I had split up with my wife; more recently, she had become my sweetheart. She had more than a dozen years of training in ballet, but now that she lives out in the desert away from ballet schools, she improvises dance routines for half an hour of exercise each night.

"I've seen Caroline when she's working through her regular routines, and it is always lovely," I went on. "But every now and then, something extraordinary happens; she calls it 'putting on her sailor's pants' because the first time it happened, she thought that her change from leotards and tights to loose-fitting navy surplus pants had something to do with her sudden buoyancy. She sailed through movements that she remembered from some Fred Astaire musical she had seen as a child. When I once caught a glimpse of her in that mode, her sensuality overwhelmed me. She was so fluid; every movement fit the mood of the music. She was lovely to see, so *fully alive* . . ."

I caught my breath, a little embarrassed. I needn't have been, for Ginger had seen the same vivacity in Caroline's dancing on several occasions. I was astonished at how vivid that memory of Caroline was—the image of her flowing through her steps. I realized that the sensuality I had seen in young Umbrian couples, the elegance in the elderly couple waltzing, the exuberance of Caroline's dance aerobics, and the elation I felt when jogging wilderness trails were all derived from the same source. They came from a rapture rooted in being fully attentive to movement, as if one's entire body were conscious, rather than just the brain. On the cliff faces that Ginger climbs, such attentiveness guarantees survival. Elsewhere in the world, it allows us not only to survive but to thrive. It is a quality that I recognized in many of the physically active Italian country people we had run into and one that I imagined Saint Francis embodied as well. I tilted my glass, watching the syrupy *grappa* shift to one side, took another drink, and felt its lingering flavor on my tongue.

"Gary, have you missed being out of touch with Caroline much during this trip?"

"I really miss her. Imagining her dancing makes me miss her more. I can't wait to be with her again."

"Always remember," Ginger said carefully, quietly, "that she is among those who have a remarkable capacity to *dance through this life*. If each of you can remember to encourage the expression of that capacity in the other, your relationship will continue to grow. Don't become one of those couples which is always *working* at their relationship; *play* at it, too!"

"Well, then, that goes for us too!" I grinned. "May we dance the trail all the way to Assisi!" We toasted the moment and downed the rest of our brandies. I two-stepped up the stairs and into my bed, where I fell under the spell of a dozen spicy dreams. In one of them, a predator came down the canyon where I was sitting; mountain lion or wolf, I could sense it stalking me. When it finally came close enough to pounce on me, I could feel that it was a fine dancer.

Chapter 5

In America, the black gold that they mine from the ground is petroleum. Here, it is truffles.

PIERLUIGI, GRADE SCHOOL STUDENT,

MONTE CASTELLO DI VIBIO

Where the Wild Things Aren't:
Truffles and Wolves

ur path rose, rambled, and smelled of another country once we crossed the Tiber River. We climbed out of the Tiber valley east of Città di Castello, toward Gubbio, the fabled land of wolves. It *was* a distinct country: truffle country. Two of the most prized edible mushrooms in the world are found together here: the white and the black truffle. Somehow we began to catch the drift of the difference that their presence made.

Not that you ever see truffles when you are out hiking around. They are as subterranean as food ever gets. And we couldn't sniff them out of the ground either; neither of us had the nose of a pointer, setter, bear, or sow.

It is said that sows are the most passionate truffle grubbers, and I pondered this as we walked along. I had been amazed to learn that white truffles contain the same substance, androstenol, as is found in the saliva of boars when they are aroused for mounting sows. Roughly twice as much of this sex hormone is found in a ripened *tartufo bianco* as scientists can find in the blood of the most virile pig. Oddly, the only other place where androstenol has been isolated is in the saliva of males of our own species. George Sand, the hedonistic French novelist of Victorian times, may have been correct in calling the truffle "the black magic apple of love."

As Ginger and I hiked along, my imagination was piqued by the notion of a plant aphrodisiac that could stimulate more than one kind of animal. Although we may have been walking right over them, neither of us sensed anything around us so persuasive as porcine sex pheromones. Unfortunately, we did not encounter any animals along the trail who were more attuned to truffle eroticism than we were.

When at last we were able to taste and see truffles, it was after they had been placed on our plates at an outrageous price. Our tangible clues to the presence of truffles in the countryside were mostly the side effects of their exorbitant value: locked gates with groves of hazelnut and oak on the other side, fenced-in nurseries where truffle inoculum had been sown, and laboratories at field stations where the mycorrhizal fungi were detached from plant roots to be cultured and purified. While the hills before us offered a hint of wildness that we had not seen near the Tiber floodplain, we gradually came to understand that even in the uplands, wildness was a scarce commodity. Surrogates were often marketed in its stead.

It was not too long after leaving the valley of the eastern Etruscans that we began to feel as though we had gotten off the beaten path. We were headed for Pietralunga, a fortified hilltop village, and had decided to strike out on the most obscure route to it that we could find. We followed single-lane gravel roads and their connecting footpaths most of the day. They grew more poorly marked the farther from the pavement we strayed.

These ancient trails looped up, around, and over ridges, past abandoned farmsteads, and through overgrown fields. Then they dropped away from signs of previous human occupancy. Gradually, forest became more common than field, and pasture more frequent than truck farms teeming with vegetables. Two hours to market by truck must be too much for a farmer to travel daily in order to sell vegetables in the closest hubs of Gubbio and Umbertide.

Much of the Umbrian countryside had been depopulated by the end of World War II, not only because of the war itself but also because agricultural mechanization had left little need for so many *contadini* on each farm. In rural areas to the north and east of where we were walking, many of the deserted houses and rundown farms had been recolonized by the nouveau riche during the last three decades. On the path we traveled, however, recolonization had not yet occurred. We took tracks that were not marked on our maps and hiked through a sparsely settled mountain range that was not so much out of reach of the landed gentry as out of mind for now.

Ginger and I spoke with relief of being out in the boonies again, for Città di Castello had made us claustrophobic with its bountiful creature comforts. We were now hoping to see land as untamed as the places Saint Francis had known— rough country where a monk could set up a hermitage in a cave and see more wildlife than people, more untamed forest than farmland. Still, we were disappointed; there simply was no sizable refuge left here that seemed essentially wild.

There was forest, yes, but it was what farmers in other parts of the world call "go-back": planted trees or volunteering shrubs fenced in an area where a field or pasture had been in the past. We saw hunters in camouflage khakis playing around on the edges of woods but heard no rumblings from within the thicker forest patches and saw no one emerge from them during the entire day. Not that the secondary forest was entirely uninviting. It was simply not large enough to hide within it many distinct microhabitats, and the birds that the hunters were after probably kept to its edges. Like the songbirds and the hunters, we too kept to its edges as we walked on.

Nevertheless, we saw only the above-ground forest, when what most interested us were signs about the subterranean one. Posted on fences were placards proclaiming "Truffle Reserve: Harvest Regulated by the State Forestry Department." Such reserves were carefully protected by high hurricane fences, and the placard on one informed us of experimental inoculations of white truffles within.

I leaned against this fence, my face pressed into its holes, my fingers wrapped around its galvanized wire. We had just come up a steep hill, and I was still panting. I peered at the oak and hazelnut saplings of uniform size, spaced evenly in neat rows.

"Pretty boring above ground," I muttered to myself. Beneath the ground, however, there was an unimaginable mess of mycelium growing in coral-like formations on tree roots. Like miniature, inverted trees, millions of brownish-red and white fungal filaments grew every which way—an anarchist's dream. This unseen forest of warty fungi was approaching the ripened edible stages of its existence.

I sniffed deeply. The subterranean fungus must be just a few feet away. I closed my eyes and imagined that it was sniffing back at me, for the surface of a truffle has the same texture as the nose of a dog. Although the hurricane fence could certainly not hold in whatever fragrances emerged from the earth, the fungal aroma remained too diffuse for me to perceive.

No one knows when Umbrians first discovered that their local truffles were both fragrant and palatable, but the old peasants speak as though it happened within their lifetime.

"It has not been all that long," suggested one old man, "that the truffle has been known to us. We were herding our pigs, trying to get them to some hills far from our village so that they could find enough plants to browse. We were moving them along when one of the pigs went crazy. He had jumped onto something we couldn't see and was foaming at the mouth over it. We ran in around him, scared that something terrible had happened. He had found a truffle.

"Well, we still did not know that we could *eat* it, until one day a man discovered a large truffle out under a tree where he had been digging for other purposes. When he had completely excavated it, the truffle gave off such a delicious perfume that he ran home and tried to cook it.

"Once it was cooked, he took a bite out of a whole truffle, but it didn't make him feel very good. Then he tried preparing it different ways, first with a large chunk of the truffle, then with a thin slice, then with a shaving, which was even better when it was mixed in with other food. In the end, he tried grating the rest of the truffle over his pasta; the flavor was out of this world."

"How long ago did this happen?" asked the old farmer's grandchild.

"Oh, at least forty-five or fifty years ago," the old man guessed. Ancient history for the child, vivid memory for him.

Surprisingly, statisticians claim that only half of the peasants in rural Umbria have tasted truffles. Independent, serendipitous discoveries of their overpowering bouquet may indeed be happening in the forest again and again, in one family or another, all the time. Yet more and more of the truffles being produced are from cultivated stands of trees rather than from wild forests.

The effort toward domesticating the black truffle began with the work of a French peasant, Joseph Talon, in 1810. As in Jean Giono's fable from Provence, *The Man Who Planted Trees*, Talon, without prompting from others, diligently planted acorns on stony, siliceous earth. Somehow, during this endeavor, he recognized a rather strong association between oaks and black truffles. He returned to his plantings year after year and finally encountered what he had been hoping for: black truffles in the ground beneath the oak duff.

According to oral history, Talon quietly took the money made from selling his truffles and plowed it back into the planting of more oak plantations wherever he guessed that the "truffle seed" might naturally occur in the soil. For decades he told no one outside his family about his understanding of this ecological interaction or about how he had nurtured it.

Then, as an old man, Talon consented to letting his cousin Rousseau spread the word about this indirect method of truffle cultivation. Following the 1855 World Exposition in Paris, this forestry technique for cultivating mushrooms became widely practiced.

Wild truffle harvests in both Italy and France probably reached their peak in the last century, when there were more eyes and feet covering rural ground than there are today. Yields from the forests have been falling along the same curve that rural population figures follow. At the same time, truffle cultivation and truffle prices show a meteoric rise. Today, a pound of fresh truffles can bring the equivalent of a thousand dollars on the retail market in London. From New Zealand to northern California, entrepreneurs are scrambling to establish truffle empires.

There remain those who simply search for truffles and related *scorzone* mushrooms in truly wild places. Food historian Elizabeth Romer has emphasized how important an economic and aesthetic activity truffle hunting is for some old men. Beth has encountered truffle hunters who are "almost sylvan in their appearance. They rarely venture into towns, perhaps once or twice a year for the large fairs or when they have something to sell. Their hands are cracked and ingrained with soil, their hair is long, and their faces are wrinkled and deep brown from the sun and wind. They have a scent of foxes and forests about them."

These peasants are faithful to secret locations where, in the past, truffles have been found on untended ground. Not far from Pietralunga, Ginger and I crossed the path of Francesco Fiorucci, a sun-cured farmer who loves truffles as much as he does his home-grown vegetables. The morning we arrived, he was taking great care in braiding together the husks of sweet corn ears and hanging them on the south side of his tractor shed to dry.

When he found that we were walking to Assisi, he exclaimed, "Francesco! He's my saint, my namesake!" And he herded us into his barnyard to share some wine from his cellar. He offered a blessing with the first drink and refilled our glasses whenever there was a break in the conversation. We asked about the white truffle.

"*Tartufi?*" he responded. "The white ones are just appearing. This year will be so-so. Not abundant rain, but not a drought either. The price might be average," he motioned with a hand wavering in the air, as if teetering on a balance, "or a little better than that. It may run anywhere from 130,000 to 400,000 lire for a pound of truffles."

He drank a glass of his raspberry-red *vino locale*, then shrugged his shoulders. "Of course, I'm not as adept at finding them in the field as my brother was. Before he died, he was the only person in our family to be fully consumed with truffle hunting—he was very diligent. He knew the places, the times. I can tell you that a black *scorzone* is just about done at this time of year, and we are ready for the white truffle, which is almost here with us. We will be taking our dogs out to find them. Pigs? Pigs haven't been used here for a while, maybe a century."

Customs have changed since 1572, when a German baron asked Giacomo Castelvetro to solve a problem that had been plaguing him since his last visit to Italy: "Can you tell me, my friend, since you are Italian, why it is that the noblemen of the most civilized nation in the world perambulate their estates in the company of pigs?"

Pigs were now out of the picture, but I remained curious about the dogs. As Italians have labored toward truffle domestication, have they also worked on selecting canine harvesters that are particularly sensitive to truffles?

"Will any dog do?" I asked.

"Pointers are ideal for the *raccolta*, the wild harvest, but other breeds will do fine if they are carefully trained. You see, truffling takes a lot of patience, both in handling the dogs and learning the forest yourself. Young men sometimes do it for the money, but it is really an art suited for old men like me."

He laughed, then added, "The only trouble is, I'm seventy-two years old and I'm still no expert!"

An old hand at truffle hunting, it is said, hardly needs a hog or dog to accompany him. He listens for the buzz of yellow truffle flies. He watches for spots below oaks where the herbs look scorched; there, the truffles below have sapped the soil of its nutrients. The ground has a subtle, moundlike rise to it, and the surface is fissured with minuscule cracks and crevices. Only a few grasses like fescue seem tolerant of such soil. Where the ground is cracked like this, some trufflers claim they can catch a whiff of the truffle's aroma once they kneel on the earth.

If such signals all emanate from the same spot, the truffler will go down on all fours and plunge his knife into the earth. By the degree of resistance he feels in his hand, he can tell whether his knife has touched truffle, rock, or root. He slides his knife down again at another angle, and with a flick of the wrist, tests to see if a ripened mushroom will pop up out of the earth. If it doesn't pop out, he digs deeper, opening up a narrow trough while looking for traces of the truffle along the cross-section. Once he finds and removes the truffle, he carefully returns the soil and oak duff to their original conditions in order to conceal the site from his competitors.

The old men may also be expert at hoodwinking unsuspecting truffle buyers. They pass off the poorer quality *scorzone* species as high-class truffles, demanding the same stiff prices from naive buyers as experienced middlemen would pay for authentic white truffles.

Every once in a while, an old truffler will even try to gain the upper hand with an experienced middleman. The elder will find a truffle one afternoon and spend hours that evening meticulously stuffing its crevices with fine gravel. The next morning, he will sell the burgeoning tuber for twice its actual weight. If he can't fool local buyers with his loaded fungus, he catches the train to Rome, where gullible restaurateurs will pay as much as 300,000 lire for a single plump, luscious truffle.

Seasoned buyers, however, have their own savvy. On the edge of Pietralunga, I had the good fortune to catch one wholesaler as he was running his route on the back roads between there and Perugia. In his early forties, he was matter of fact about his business.

"The white truffles are starting to ripen now, yes, but

they are very fragile at this stage and difficult to ship. Better to let them wait and solidify, if you can afford it."

"Afford it?"

"Yes, I mean take the risk that someone else might harvest them in the meantime. It takes *fortuna*, luck, as well as skill. You may walk over a fairy ring of truffles early in the season and never notice it beneath you. A week later, someone else's dog may come along to where you have been and hit upon a ready harvest. Or you may fail to find them at the proper time and they will rot. At least when they rot, they resow themselves."

I guessed that this man might know whether certain dogs are being bred exclusively for truffle hunting. I angled in on the topic.

"So a good dog will help you find the truffles before they rot?"

"Oh, yes." He sat sideways on the seat of his sports car, legs stretched out in the sun, and smiled. He liked dogs. "With the dogs, you know, it is something in the bloodline. Brack pointers do best, but it is not just a matter of the breed alone. The progeny of expert pointers seem to retain their parent's ability if it is not wasted by lack of training when they are young."

"What age of dog is best for truffling?"

"Well, as they reach six or seven, they begin to calm down a bit in the presence of truffles, instead of acting so frenzied. Before that age, truffles too strongly command their bodies. You must be strong to pull a young dog off them. You literally have to jerk them off the ground to keep them from digging and mauling the truffle."

There was a pause. He tucked his feet into the car and

prepared to leave for his next purchasing stop. He closed the car door and winked. "It *is* the aphrodisiac they say it is. It will command the body of a man or woman just as it will command the body of a dog or pig."

With that, he drove off, knowing that the best way to promote his product was to plant the seeds of its enigmatic qualities in a libidinous imagination.

I stood there for a while, entranced, wondering if I could breed better Brack pointers. If I had the chance, I would try selecting for sires that might have tidal waves of androstenol splashing through their bloodstream. And if the dogs weren't blessed with the same pheromone that humans and hogs have, perhaps they could sense another as yet undescribed fragrance given off by truffles.

Either way, it is fortunate that such provocative substances are found in fungi hidden in the Italian earth and not in every pharmacy within the urban centers of the world. An earthy aphrodisiac cut loose from its context could wreak more havoc on the planet than could a dozen atom bombs.

After a night at a ski lodge near Pietralunga, Ginger and I hiked to Gubbio, where we entered store after store advertising a bewildering litany of exotic-sounding truffle products: *grappa norcina al tartufo nero di Noccia; olio tartufato; tartufi acqualagna; pate di quaglia tartufato; formaggio Waiter al tartufo; amaro al tartufo nero*; and *tartufella porcini e tartufo bianco*. It seemed like everything in sight was spiked, seeded, soaked, or cured with truffles: flavored brandies and olive oils; curdled cheese spreads; hard cheeses with truffles embedded within them; bitters of black truffles; and pickled truffles with *porcini* mushrooms.

Truffle hunting has even become a spectator sport. For 80,000 lire per person, we could have gone out with a vanload of tourists to take pictures of a local expert digging truffles with his own dog. Or one could wait until November, when the gourmet chefs would come into town for the Seventh Annual "Truffles Today" Congress. I began to get the feeling that truffle hysteria had become as boring and lucrative for native Umbrians as the blackened redfish craze is for Cajuns or blue corn blintzes are for New Mexicans.

If there is a difference, it is in the manner that truffles are dished out: a little can go a long way. For lunch in Gubbio, we began with black truffle brochettes and moved on to tagliatelle with asparagus and mushrooms, ravioli and eggplant. Over the whole meal—and for that matter, throughout the rest of the day and evening—the fine lingering taste of sautéed truffle shavings held my tongue, nose, and throat in rapture.

Later, while out on my own, I finally tracked down a restaurant that had just received its first white truffles for the year. They weren't yet listed on the menu; the only listed truffle dish was the same brochette with truffle shavings that Ginger and I had shared. I corralled the senior waiter.

"Is it possible to have truffles fixed any other way here at your restaurant?" I asked, as politely as I could. "I have a special interest in wild foods, and I was wondering . . ."

"Signore, you are in luck! That is, if you don't mind eating something that is not listed on our menu as yet. I believe that the head cook has two ways of fixing the white truffles we just got this morning. Let me speak with him."

He returned. "Would you prefer to have the white truffle shavings sautéed in butter with tortellini or to have them blended with bread crumbs and scattered over linguini?"

I paused, then asked about the tortellini. He explained that they were stuffed with veal, prosciutto, and Parmesan cheese. After this mouth-watering description, it was difficult for me to imagine how the truffles could be as intense if blended with bread crumbs.

"*Desidero tortellini in burro fuso con tartufo bianco, per favore,*" I announced.

When he reappeared, the waiter transported a bowl still hot to the touch, with the sizzle of butter rising from its midst. The pale shavings of truffles carried a smoky, woody scent. The tortellini were golden and nearly translucent after their dive into the heated butter.

I savored every bite, keeping the flavors in my mouth as long as I could. All too quickly my bowl was empty.

The waiter instantly reappeared after the last morsel had been washed down with wine.

"Anything else for you, sir?"

"What could there be that would complement the truffles?"

"Did you say you have a special interest in wild foods, something from the *cucina regionale*, perhaps? There are one or two items on the menu that would normally do, but we have a momentary shortage of the customary ingredients. You see, the catch is just beginning."

"The catch?"

He paused. "Yes, the catch. We would not have enough to provide you with a full plate of thrushes, but would you be willing to settle for a mix of songbirds?"

A lump came to my throat. I had not expected to meet wild biological diversity face to face at the dinner table. Saint Francis, have mercy on me . . .

Those truffles had a taste, like that of bird peppers or venison, so essentially wild that it conjured up for me the thought of ancient foods from our Paleolithic past. Still, I could not tell by taste whether a truffle was truly from the wild or from laboratory stock seeded in a hazelnut plantation. Of course, few of my fellow tourists at the Gubbio restaurants would have known or even cared that an ever-increasing percentage of the truffles were coming from cultivated plots. Watching the purchases pile high on the counters at the specialty markets, I realized that I was possibly alone in my fear that domesticating the truffle might eventually degrade its wild flavor, as has happened with so many other domestications.

My first assumption—that the truffles I ate had been taken from the wild—may have been an erroneous one. The Italian Society for Forestry and Agriculture has helped in-oculate truffles in more than fifty experimental plots covering over 275 acres. Within these plots—like the one where my nose poked through a hole in the hurricane fence—foresters have transplanted more than 40,000 oaks, hazelnuts, poplars, and willows. These trees were raised in sterile soil and fed artificial fertilizers. Once established, they were "seeded" with the inocula from either *Tuber melanosporum*, the black truffle, or *Tuber magnatum*, the white.

The inoculation of soil with mycorrhizal fungal spores remains a crapshoot, a speculation in which only the daring and the rich can indulge. Success depends on locating plots containing soil of the proper alkalinity, texture, and, perhaps, geological history. Anyone going into the plots is required to wear sterilized suits and boots, for fear that the inoculated earth might become contaminated with fungal competitors. If black truffle spores happen to invade the site, they will outcompete the more valuable white tubers. Even under the most antiseptic, controlled conditions, some plots simply refuse to bear. Most of the Forestry Society's biologists have retained a certain humility. They honestly admit that even they can't predict which trees will produce tuber harvests and which won't.

"Maybe in a hundred, two hundred years, truffle growing will be reliable. Maybe by then we will have a pointer-setter cross that will be *the* dog especially evolved for truffle hunting. But for now, it is *fortuna* as much as *abilità*—how do you say 'precise skill'?"

Still, lab scientists are proceeding with the taming of "the wild bunch," the mycelia that have kept the secret underground for all these millennia. Beware the day that truffle domestication is completed, when all production will depend on some precise science, rather than on some rustic talent. The following day, they may be leading you around by pheromone sprays, and the spontaneity that has enriched human sexual intimacy for two million years may be replaced by the chemical engineering of desire.

While Ginger and I had been pressing toward Gubbio, we realized that the balance between the wild and the tamed had already been tipped. Quarries lined the ridge east of the valley. The mountains above these gashes were pastured, cultivated, or mined clear up to their tops. Monte Ingino, the tutelary peak just above Gubbio's walls, was as urbanized as the village below, with trams, cafés, and a museum hooked onto the Basilica of San Ubaldo. Now, each spring, the strongest men in the village form teams to race three twenty-four-foot candles on massive wooden frames up the steep mountainside to the basilica from the village below. "Conquer the mountain" has become the biggest spectator sport in Gubbio.

The prevailing domestication of Gubbio left me a little heartbroken, for I had expected to see remnants of the untamed hinterlands of the thirteenth century. If these were the wildest habitats that could still be found in Umbria, then I had little to hope for. The mountains rose high to the east of town, but the impressive wilderness found there at the time of Saint Francis had been laid to rest. With it went the wolves and untold other animals that required at least a mix of wild and cultivated habitats.

Wildlife it lacked, but Gubbio did have its live wires. A firecracker of a woman named Emilia Valenti took Ginger and me beyond the walls of Old Gubbio to a small country chapel on the Roman road to Assisi. There, where cobblestones marked the way, she brought us to Viale della Vittorina.

"Here," she nodded toward the chapel, "is where the wolf and Francis came together. Do you know the story?"

"We would love to hear it from someone who lives here," Ginger responded.

"Well, it was in the winter and very, very cold. There was little left to eat in the country after such harsh weather.

"A she-wolf came down into the town, and she was

ferocious, completely wild. All the people of Gubbio stayed locked up in their houses, afraid to venture out in the streets.

"But when they heard that Francesco would be traveling here to visit some of his friends, they asked for his help. 'You are good with animals,' they pleaded, 'please go to the wolf and talk to her.' So Francesco came to this place where the wolf already was, and when he spoke to her, the wolf deferred to him with a gesture like this . . ."

She offered us a discreet bow in her well-fitting black dress. Her body dipped and she glanced up at us.

"Like genuflecting?"

"Yes, like that. She was tame from then on. The people would bring her a piece of meat, any animal flesh they could find, and she would live on that."

We lingered for half an hour or so, going into the small stone chapel, not much bigger today than when it was built in 853. We wondered about the claim that a wolf's skull had been excavated from beneath the chapel floor, since archaeologists had recently argued that no such skull had ever been presented to them for positive identification. We picked up garbage in the park across the way, and then, as the light began to fade, we accompanied our hostess back into the stone-walled confines of Old Gubbio.

The next day we wandered around the village for hours before climbing up Monte Ingino. All the while, my mind was spinning backward to that chapel, on a street now called Brother Wolf's Way, one block down from Gandhi's Way. I felt a sorrow there, as if what had once made this place special were now among the most remote of possibilities. If a wolf arrived here today, it would be run down by the speeding cars before anyone would notice that it was not a dog.

Today when the wolf story is told as part of the Franciscan fables, it is characteristically claimed that the saint "tamed" the beast, as if wolves should exist only if they become friendly and nonpredatory. The "bedtime story" renditions of Franciscan parables often feature the saint bringing wildlife under his spell, silencing the chattering of birds and evicting ants from places where he wishes his followers to sit and listen to him. The moral of such stories is simple: "good" animals, like "good" children, should suppress their "animal nature" and behave obediently so that their brother Francis and his heavenly father can love them.

But Francesco di Bernardone himself scored high on wild behavior and low on obedience; in fact, he is considered by many social historians to be the initiator of civil disobedience and conscientious objection against war in the Western tradition. When I put together the many pieces of the puzzle known to us as Saint Francis, I wonder why the stories have not stuck with the older inscriptions that claim only that he *made peace* with the wolf.

This reading is consistent with other Franciscan parables, not only those dealing with animals. When Francis participated in the Crusades, he wandered into the camp of the Egyptian sultan Malik al-Kamil, who at first wanted to convert Francis to Islam as badly as Francis wanted him to embrace Christianity. Over several days they exchanged views of the world, and mutual respect grew. When the sultan invited Francis to a mosque, Francis specified that he would go only as long as he was allowed to pray to *his* God there; nevertheless, the experience of someone else's holy place moved him. "God is everywhere," he conceded; even beyond Christianity in the hearts of those he formerly believed to be the enemy. These "enemies" allowed Francis to travel safely back to the camps of Christian crusaders, whose drive to defeat the Muslims no longer interested him. Francis could see no need to ask such men as his host to abandon their culture or means of worship. Likewise, ten years later, Malik al-Kamil peacefully handed Jerusalem over to Frederick the Second, avoiding the shedding of another drop of blood.

Somewhat similarly, when a widow from the wealthy Frangipani family took Francis in as a houseguest in Rome, he nicknamed her Brother Jacopa, and she became his lifelong friend. He frequently let her indulge him with almond cream cakes and other comforts, rather than enforcing his brand of poverty on her. Because he could be himself with her and not be expected to instruct her on how to be, their mutual respect held firm right up until his death, when she arrived just in time to bid Francis farewell.

Thus, when Francis called the wild canine "Brother Wolf," he was not anthropomorphizing or coaxing the creature into becoming a pet, pal, or playmate. He was simply extending his sense of community beyond the human population. When he said, "I want to make peace between you and them," I doubt that Francis wished for the wolf to become a tofu-eating vegetarian or to huddle, doglike, in the shadows of barns and houses. Perhaps the only means of making peace with someone else is by respecting his or her intrinsic nature.

Paw in hand—the gesture, of course, was a symbolic bridge between human compassion and "the other." At that time, "the other" was not merely a ferocious canid but our own animal nature in its darkest and most evil forms. An Italian medical text from 1566 describes the terrible conditions associated with *lycanthropy*, a madness that causes a person to believe that he or she is being transformed into a werewolf: "Those who are afflicted with lycanthropy, leaving their houses at night, imitate wolves in every way and, until the arrival of daylight, wander mostly about the gravestones. They are noted to be characterized by the following: pale face, eyesight weak and dry, tongue very arid, saliva lacking in the mouth, and an excessive thirst."

Ornithological theologian Edward Armstrong reminds us that both real wolves and werewolves were persecuted in Italy because of their diabolical associations: "Not only were evil individuals in the Middle Ages regarded as wolfish but wolves were sometimes treated as if they were wicked men."

It is this fear of our dark side—and the lack of acceptance of the nature of animals—that Saint Francis may have been attempting to confront. Barry Lopez sees the Gubbio parable as one of resolution between the spiritual and visceral components of our own nature. While writing *Of Wolves and Men*, Lopez may have cracked the kernel of this story: "Medieval men believed that they saw in wolves a reflection of their own bestial nature; man's longing to make peace with the beast in himself is what makes this tale of the Wolf at Gubbio one of the more poignant stories of the Middle Ages. To have compassion for the wolf, whom man saw as enslaved by the same base drives as himself, was to yearn for self-forgiveness."

If the reading by Lopez is correct, Francis did not tame

the wolf so much as he offered the Gubbini a means of seeing the wild as something more than dark, ferocious, and dangerous. He also offered them a new vision of their own complexities, complexities that medieval folk did not necessarily wish to face: the ambivalence in themselves and in other animals as well.

It may have been that medieval Europe was not ready for such a message: that we would be better off to accept our own animal nature and to allow some distance, if not coexistence, with other animals so that they too might survive. Francis and his friends, by virtue of the amount of time they spent on the margins of society, may have had more contact with wild animals such as wolves than most Italians; certainly this could have led to a tolerance of their presence that was rare compared to the fears of most medieval peasants. Still, even if Francis could muster up no real compassion for a predator among his contemporaries, perhaps the seeds of tolerance were sown.

Yet the ultimate issue is not whether one tames or makes peace with one wolf that has ventured out of the mountain wilderness. Instead, it is this: wolf populations remain viable in so few places on the Italian peninsula today precisely because the balance of wild and cultivated habitats no longer serves their needs. The habitat mosaic has been progressively simplified by the reduction in the size of wild patches and the enlargement of mechanized farmlands.

The place where Francis supposedly met the wolf is now a suburban street corner, apartment buildings on three of its four sides. Monte Ingino above it has been shorn, bald as a Benedictine monk. The forests have been cleared or agronomically engineered. This has left hardly enough cover for hares or deer, let alone for predators. The most successful way to tame a wolf is to tame her habitat.

Predators, we now know, are the scarcest and most misunderstood of all minorities. They can be quickly impoverished by disrupting or simplifying the food web on which they depend. Convert an oak savanna to maize or tobacco fields and the resident populations of herbivores will collapse or become skewed toward seed-eating mice. As a result, predators other than kestrels and a few small owls may disappear altogether.

Francis had an empathy for the endangered. He tried to grant himself no more power to wield in the world than was available to the poorest of the poor: lepers, serfs, flies, and wolves. He was not the kind to be content hanging around a garden birdbath while the world was losing its rangiest wolves and rarest wilderness.

The three hundred or so stray wolves left in Italy are still seen now and then from Genoa to Calabria, all along the Apennine range. Biologist Luigi Boitani, who has devoted his life to their conservation and study, estimates that wolves may still range over 5,750 square miles of Italy, but they maintain "no particular density in Umbria; indeed, the Gubbio area has wolves very sporadically." Yet the story of Francis taming the wolf is big business in Gubbio, even though the Gubbini have spared no wolves nor habitat for them for quite some time. Gubbio curio shops sell wolf memorabilia in volumes that parallel their sales of truffle products. It is sad that they do not invest some of their wolf-story profits into reestablishing a habitat mosaic where healthy wolf populations could recolonize, a mosaic that would include scrublands as well as pastures and fields where farmers would be compensated should wolves inflict any economic damage on livestock or crops. The closest such habitat is now more than 180 miles away from Gubbio in the Abruzzo National Park.

"No, no, they have not been seen in my lifetime," said Francesco Fiorucci, looking down at the cobblestone floor of his barn, a dozen miles from Gubbio. "In all my life, there has been no chance for me to see them."

He kicked at the straw on the floor. Then he looked up at us, remembering something, his eyes brightening. "But once, just a few years before I was born—it would have been around 1913—my grandfather saw wolves. He said it was so cold that winter, hardly any wildlife was left in the mountains. The wolves came down hungry. It was then that my grandfather lost a huge ox to seven wolves. Seven of them struck together."

He caught his breath and turned to look out the barn door. "Now, no *lupi*, not even one *lupo*. I don't know when I will die and go to heaven, but I don't expect to see a wolf before then."

Knowing that, we felt no need to stay near Gubbio any longer. We turned our sights southward to Assisi, not knowing what the mountains between might hold.

Interlude 5
Coming Full Circle

rom Gubbio, we walked out of the valley and into the rugged uplands, heading toward Assisi to the south. Past Ponte d'Assi, Ginger and I began climbing up and up on the paved road toward Perugia, then we veered off the asphalt onto muddy roads around Monte Salce. We knew that we had a place to stay for the night near Valdichiasco, but we remained unclear which mountain road led to it and what the

conditions there would be like. The lack of traffic in the backwoods left us with no one from whom we could ask directions.

Finally, a young family in a four-wheel-drive Land Rover assured us that we were on the correct route. We soon came to a small farm, where we were offered rooms in a medieval tower. Sorry, our Swiss hostess said flatly, she could not offer us any food or wine at this time of year; the nearest stores were back on the road to Gubbio.

After an hour of settling in and walking around the orchards, I decided to jog back to the pavement in order to purchase enough food for the evening and for the last leg to Assisi; otherwise, we had only a little fruit and a few crackers to last us more than twenty miles. I stripped down to jogging shorts, running shoes, and a T-shirt, and I carried a collapsible net bag so that I wouldn't be heavily burdened on the three miles back to the store. The exhilaration of a good run would be welcome after trudging up the hills like a pack animal earlier in the day. I jogged away unencumbered, but I was unprepared for the coolness of the coming nightfall, with its attendant drizzle and fog.

When I returned, soaked, a little over an hour later—with olives, unleavened bread, cheese, wine, and pesto in tow—the cold had penetrated to my bones. I immediately headed to the bathroom, left my drenched clothes in a puddle on the floor, and took a steamy shower. My fingers still felt numb when I reentered the room where Ginger had set out some dinner for us, and I went to bed right after eating, fearing that a cold might be coming on.

When I awoke in the morning, I immediately felt that something was missing. It was disturbing because I could not identify what that absence was. Ginger and I began to hike southeastward before dawn, descending a long, foggy mountain slope, and I felt troubled all the way down. As the sun's silhouette in the mist rose above another slope in front of us, I finally figured out what was wrong.

"Oh, no, Ginger, I've lost the ring that Caroline gave me. My fingers have felt odd ever since last night, but I thought it was just the numbness. Maybe the ring slipped off while I was jogging in the rain. I have to go back!"

The ring was a simple silver band that had been shaped by a desert-dwelling friend of ours who was in his eighties. This was the first time I'd had it off my hand since Caroline had given it to me a few months before. She had arranged for Julian to hammer out matching silver bands for us, not as an immediate prelude to getting married—neither of us felt ready for that—but as a way to celebrate our growing relationship. Now, feeling its absence reminded me of another time. When my ex-wife and I split up, I had rid myself of the wedding ring I had worn since the day of our marriage, and I had not worn any jewelry for another two years. The sudden loss of this ring made me feel empty again, the way I had that day I'd cut my wedding ring in half and tossed it into an irrigation ditch—so much water under the bridge.

"Go back to the tower and look around," Ginger said. "Leave your pack, and I'll go through things here."

I raced up the slopes, panting, my second fogged-in run back to the tower in twelve hours. When I arrived back in Valdichiasco, our hostess was bewildered, but after I explained my dilemma, she gave me the keys to the tower. I scoured the floors, the beds, the trash cans, and sinks—no ring. If I had lost it, it had probably been on the run the night before.

No doubt it was among the mud and weeds somewhere on the three miles of dirt road between here and the market. I gave up.

As I jogged back to where Ginger had stayed with the packs, I was crestfallen. It was not so much the ring itself, I thought, but the bond I felt with Caroline—I didn't want to lose *that*. She would roll her eyes when I told her what had happened, then forgive me for losing the ring under difficult circumstances, but suddenly I realized how precious her presence in my life had become. The ring was just a superficial manifestation of the potential of our partnership, yet until it was gone from my hand, I had not thought about how vulnerable such a partnership could be if not given constant attention. This travel time away from Caroline and from my children and my desert home meant that none was being given the full attention that it deserved. I had suffered one failure for such reasons; my spirit could not afford another.

For me, as for many adventurous men of present and past generations, trekking had come to mean freedom from the shackles of domestic life, a chance to make contact with wildness again. Whenever I had felt the conflicts and constraints of my previous marriage, I would simply dream up an expedition into the wilderness to take the pressure off our relationship—or so I supposed. Yet there is something fundamentally faulty with this polarity of wildness being "out there"—beyond relationship—and domestication being the only kind of long-term intimacy we allow with another person, plant, or animal. Under such a structure, no wonder marriages become impoverished; no wonder couples lose the "wildness" of sexuality that they first felt with one another;

no wonder family ties are seen as static and confining rather than as fluid connections.

But there is another way to structure our view of the world: the concepts of home, family, and community do not need to be opposed to the concepts of wildness and expressiveness. As my friend Terry Tempest Williams has said of the landscape of marriage, couples must "open the bedroom doors at night, and invite the wild creatures in." If we begin to consider the most intimate and continual relationships we have with others as the most wild and the most fundamental to our biological well-being, then the conflicts caused by the old polarities vanish. In this view, the ring that I place on my finger is no longer a shackle but a connector, a symbol of ever-widening circles of relationship.

My strides were reaching over a yard wide as I sailed down the last mountain slope to where Ginger stood. She smiled at me, then opened her hand.

"May I interest you in a silver ring?" She giggled. "It must have slipped from your cold hand when you came back and took a shower last night, but it ended up in the bottom of the bag with your towel and toilet kit. Well, my absent-minded friend, I hope you enjoyed your run—I enjoyed my time on the mountainside, basking in the fog. How *are* you doing?"

"Oh, I don't know . . . I was pretty torn up about losing the ring. What a relief! *Thank you* for your help. Should we begin walking again?"

"I'm ready to dance the Franciscan Way, if you are . . ."

"Ginger," I said as I put on the ring, then the backpack,

"I think I figured out why the pope agreed to let Francis establish his orders as part of the church, rather than having him burned as a heretic."

She looked at me in a funny way. "This is what you thought about while searching for your ring?"

"No, it just dawned on me. The pope must have worried that the Catholic church was threatened by becoming too formal, too inbred, too much a closed community, too tame. Rather than fighting with the wild-eyed prophets on the fringes, he welcomed Francis into the church in order to renew it. And Francis, feeling that the church had opened up to him, opened that sense of community even wider, to include wild creatures as well. Without embracing that influx of wildness, Western civilization would have died right there and then, just like a crop that has become too genetically uniform. So maybe the pope and Saint Francis really weren't at odds at all. They just had different vantage points, like an eagle and a wolf stalking the same land."

"Takes two to tango," Ginger said. "Let's foxtrot down this trail so we have a chance of reaching Assisi by dusk. Then maybe I can begin to picture this wild-eyed Francis guy in his place."

I touched the ring on my finger, and my feet went into motion, touching the ground.

Chapter 6

Once upon a time there were some woods, a footpath, and a little chapel, almost completely in ruins. The woods have been replaced by a city, the path by a road, and over the chapel stands a mighty basilica. It is useless to regret these changes; in a way, they help remind us that contemporary spirituality does not permit us to return to the pristine days of Franciscan living.

P. THÉOPHILE DESBONNETS

Hands on the Land:
Grape Raisers and Bean Eaters

he roads between Gubbio and Valfabricca rose up into Umbrian hill country that was as full of pattern as any land I had ever seen. As we danced along the trail, I finally began to notice these designs—where different plants and human activities fit against the slopes, saddles, and summits of the rolling terrain; where orchards were protected from fierce winds and late freezes; where houses, barns, and pastures were

nestled for warmth in the winter; where vineyards thrived, surviving a record-breaking freeze within the last decade; and where even fields of annuals could be sown without significant erosion.

Grain fields, for instance, were usually placed on the most gently sloping hillsides, while drainage ways and out-crops surrounded by thin soils were always kept wooded so that the forest litter slowed runoff to a halt. Houses were perched on natural balconies, just below the ridge tops. Per-manent pastures were on the roughest land that was too steep or poor to support fields or orchards. Exhausted grain fields were being converted to vineyards and to plantations of oak and hazelnut for truffle production, since these don't demand as many nutrients as the annual crops had, year in and year out, until they had worn out the soil fertility.

I worried whenever I thought of the demands made by summer annual crops imported from the New World, for they have evolved on a richer diet of nitrogen than has been possible here for perhaps over a thousand years. Nothing looked so sad to me as ten thousand undernourished sun-flower hybrids with their heads bowed and their stalks with-ered, praying to the sun for more sustenance from the soil. When we walked by such hungry stands of annuals, we heard no sound except a futile rattling in the dry wind.

In contrast, when we passed by perennial hedges, or-chards, and vineyards, there was a resounding chorus in the air. A community of insects and birds well accustomed to these ancient crops reverberated with the energy of olive and grape, peaking in abundance just before the *vendemmia*, the vintage harvest.

To grasp such designs, I had needed nearly ten days of

ambling along, immersed in this tapestry, like a weaver's needle winding up and over, down and under the yarn already in place. What was so different to me about this land was that human weavers themselves had been deftly integrated into the fabric. Centuries of peasant farmers toiled to embellish the natural patchwork of soils, solar exposures, and storm courses in order to situate themselves, their beasts, and seeds in the paths of least resistance.

Gradually, each patch has been dyed a color different from that of its former natural cover but one that matches its current qualities: gold for the grain and straw; purple and pale green for the vineyard; sulphur yellow for the oilseeds; blacks, reds, and greens mixed in the hedgerows' brambles; grayish green for the olive trees, with forage legumes spreading beneath them.

Although the sunflowers and hybrid maizes were not grown here in the days of the early Franciscans, something akin to this living, breathing quiltwork must have covered the hills and comforted the soul of young Francesco di Bernardone. His aesthetics and ethics were somehow embedded in this notion of "not man apart," as liberation theologian Leonardo Boff suggests:

> *Here is made clear a distinct way of being-in-the-world, not over things, but together with them, like brothers and sisters of the same family. . . . It is not a dead and inanimate universe; things are not tossed here, within the reach of possessive appetites of hunger; nor are they placed beside one another. They are alive and have their own personality; they have blood ties to humanity. And because they are brothers and sisters, they cannot be violated, but rather must be respected. It is from this that Saint Francis,*

surprisingly, but consistent with his nature, prohibits the brothers
from cutting any tree at the roots, that they may bud again. He
commanded the gardeners to leave a plot of uncultivated land so
that all types of grasses might grow, including weeds, because
"they too proclaim the beauty of the Father in all things." He
also wanted, in the orchards, together with the vegetables and
fruit trees, flowers and aromatic herbs to be grown "so that all
who contemplate them may be drawn to eternal sweetness."

Here was a vision of a world worked and nurtured by
the generations of humans who have been among its inhabitants, a world that has been made sweeter by them. As
D. H. Lawrence asserted, human cultures "*can* live on the
earth and by the earth without disfiguring the earth. It has
been done here, on all these sculptured hills and softly,
sensitively terraced slopes." As I walked, I could see that
some resources had obviously been used, but much had been
given back. There were as many or more signs of renewal as
there were signs of elimination. Certain patches had been
left for the brambles, birds, hops, and herbs that spiced the
larder so that a measure of wildness stayed within reach. This
aesthetic seemed so deeply, so anciently ingrained in Umbrian
landscapes that it was now hard for me to imagine them
without footprints worn into the rocky trails or without
ancient trees pruned into shapes I would never find in a
virgin forest.

Yet as Ginger and I pushed closer to Assisi, we saw fewer
and fewer hands or feet out on the land, reinforcing that
ancient imprint. Between 1951 and 1981, the number of
peasants farming and herding in small mountain villages between Gubbio and Assisi had been reduced by half, as the

relationship between the back country and the larger economy shifted. Resorts and retreats for urbanites have replaced many of the working farms. Other rural families have reduced the variety of their crops and no longer run diversified farms. Instead, they supplement their income with bed-and-breakfast "agritourism" lodges, having refurbished their barns and the former quarters of their farmhands to serve as guest rooms.

It is not surprising that tractors have all but replaced draft animals for plowing. Even though Italian tractors are more compact and better suited to small fields, there has still been a tendency to combine two or three garden-sized patches into one larger sweep. Hedgerows have been culled out where tractors require more room to turn around and where roads have been paved and widened. I particularly resented the demise of hedges, for the few stretches of trail where we had walked alongside them were the best for both bird watching and berry eating. I kept imagining Franciscan friars from centuries before gorging themselves on the raspberries and other fruits that lined the Strada Francescana. In fact, I had wondered whether the routes they chose reflected the best trajectories for continuous foraging, where living fencerows, hedgerows, and windbreaks were kept in the richest condition. The extant hedges in central Italy probably provide some of the best habitat for migratory songbirds that it has left.

Today, the Strada Francescana's fruit supply was dwindling for other reasons. Orchards placed too far from markets and homes had not been pruned, weeded, or picked. Ancient stone walls had fallen down, so livestock had been able to get into orchards and hedges and do their damage. There were simply fewer hands keeping the old stone fences in place. And concrete posts had all but replaced wooden poles or living trees as uprights in the vineyards.

In only one place between Gubbio and Assisi did I spot living trees serving as trelliswork for grapevines—an ancient practice referred to as *opio*, once common throughout northern and central Italy. Traditionally, hedge maples or elms were pruned to branch upward, then outward near their tops, setting up a living espalier for the spread of the vines within reach of the pickers. On one north-facing hillside, I saw an *opio* planting of dwarf maples and grapes, coupled together every twenty paces like partners onstage in some ballet. I asked a local resident about them; he was surprised that I even cared.

"Maples are better than other trees for the *opio*," the elderly Umbrian farmer told me. "Less shade, less fighting with the other trees' roots in the earth."

"So it still works well?"

"Oh, yes," he replied.

"Do others still trellis grapes this way?" I wondered.

"Not here," he said, flatly. "Of this, there is no more."

On all the other farms within sight of this one instance of the old *opio* way of companion planting, the grapevines danced alone, twining around towering concrete posts and wire.

After witnessing the modernization of the rural Italian landscape, many observers would concede that Desbonnets, in the epigraph at the beginning of this chapter, is correct; it is useless to regret such changes. Aren't romantics the only ones who would favor the aesthetic qualities of the living trellis over the concrete? Who could economically justify the constant pruning and tending of the maples, when post-and-wire support for the grapes hardly costs a cent after its installment?

But the favoring of dead technology over the living has its ecological as well as its aesthetic costs. Near Venice, some insect ecologists have found enough remaining vineyards where hedge maples support grapes to compare their health with that of dead-support vineyards. They wanted to gain a sense of how insect pests respond to this 3,500-year-old companionship between maple and grape.

They found that hedge maples serve as a haven of greenery for predatory mites—insects that prey on grape pests—during winter and spring months when no leaves have sprouted on the vines. The presence of the maples keeps the mites abundant for most of the year so that these predators can begin to control pests before their numbers reach epidemic proportions on the grape crop. Because six different kinds of mites move back and forth between grape and maple, this community of predators offers a resilience to the hedge-maple vineyards that cannot be found where concrete posts or dry stakes are used as uprights.

"It is the union of the maple and the vine," commented Monica Babetto, "that serves as the place of refuge and diffusion for the beneficial species." Babetto and her ecological colleagues go one step further, affirming that compared to concrete posts, the companion plants "offer greater stability to the vineyard's agricultural ecosystem."

Be that as it may, hard-line economists care little about ecological stability in agriculture as long as a cropping method returns profits in the short term. What they care about even less is the distinction between traditional and exotic crops.

Why not simply grow the varieties that can yield the most money by the most expedient means?

What struck me about the Umbrian hill country was that most of its farmers still preferred to grow traditional crops over more profitable exotic hybrids, regardless of how modern and mechanized their farming methods had become. These farmers still kept 55,000 acres in vineyards and 68,000 acres in olive orchards, as well as nearly 20,000 acres in a mixture of other food crops. Legumes, including garden beans and fava beans, remain among the top vegetable crops in Umbria. So many beans are grown and consumed by Umbrians that they have long been called the *mangia-fagioli,* or "bean eaters."

One could justify the emphasis on grapes and olives from a strictly economic viewpoint, for wine and oil are commodities with high cash value. Beans are not. Yet when I first came to Assisi in 1990, I had been struck by the amount of land devoted to favas, the legume known to the British as broad beans, of "Jack and the Beanstalk" fame. It seemed to me then that every patch of cultivated ground, from field-sized plots to the smallest backyard garden, had its share of rows reserved for the upright plants of favas. The same had been true as one traveled southward in Italy, clear to Sicily and Sardinia.

Fava beans have developed an incredibly strong following among Italians, one that cannot be explained by their economic value to farmers or, for that matter, by their taste to consumers. Instead, they are an example of a traditional crop having subtle, long-term survival value for an ethnic group, thus demonstrating without a doubt that such an "uneconomic" allegiance to a traditional food is neither superstitious nor maladaptive. In fact, Italians have been genetically selected to favor a certain level of fava bean consumption in order to protect them from a recurrent disease in the Mediterranean—malaria.

To understand the genetic bond between favas and Italians, I had to learn something of malaria. Malaria has been one of the major killers in the Mediterranean over the millennia; at least four major waves of this epidemic have washed over Italy since Roman times. Even though international health organizations claim that they wiped out malaria in Europe and its adjacent islands by 1960, there has recently been a minor resurgence of it; no pathogen is vanquished so easily.

The parasite responsible for malaria spends one phase of its life cycle in anopheline mosquitoes, found in marshes or in pools of irrigation tailwaters, and another in the human bloodstream. Italy's bouts with malaria always raged worst along the marshy coasts of the Tyrrhenian Sea, but the disease seemed to spread wherever large-scale farming sought to divert rivers into holding ponds and ditches. Periodically irrigated fields and their ponds of tailwater functioned much like marshes from a mosquito's point of view. Wherever feudal landowners irrigated massive tracts of pasture or field crop in Tuscany or Umbria, they left enough standing water in their wake to let malaria enter. As one of the first ecological historians has put it, malaria and feudalism collaborated to shape the demography of Mediterranean Europe: "It is characteristic of malaria," claimed L. W. Hackett, "to exploit troubled situations and help round out vicious circles."

All the while malaria was periodically devastating Mediterranean agricultural communities, however, its survivors were slowly accumulating a measure of genetic resistance to it. Malaria had an increasingly tougher time completing its vicious cycle, because human dwellers along the Mediterranean were developing a genetic response that reduced their vulnerability to the disease.

Italians and their neighbors developed a curious genetic deficiency of a particular enzyme that doctors now know by the glamorous name of "G6PD." This deficiency kept malaria parasites from growing well in red blood cells where oxygen was limited. If the parasite could not find the tremendous amount of oxygen it needed, it died early rather than reproducing and infecting the liver of its human victim.

Human geneticists sometimes call the G6PD deficiency the most common genetic "disorder" in the world—more common than sickle-cell anemia. It is shared by well over 100 million people, primarily those of ethnic groups derived from malaria-stricken parts of the Mediterranean and Africa. Until recently, it has been called a disorder, because males with G6PD deficiency can develop a severe anemia triggered by certain unusual conditions. This anemia is brought on by certain infections, by taking the antimalarial drug primaquine, by eating *Morchella* mushrooms, by eating an abundance of raw fava beans, or by inhaling large doses of pollen from fava flowers.

Thus, at first glance, it would appear that genetically deficient Italians should stay as far away from fava beans as possible. Eating fava beans or snorting fava pollen is like pulling the trigger on a loaded genetic gun: what a *maladaptive* thing for Italians to do! Favas can cause them sickness or death, thereby keeping Italians from passing on the very genes that could protect their future generations from malaria. It is no wonder that they developed certain taboos in order to put a lid on excessive fava bean consumption.

One such taboo, forbidding touching fresh favas or setting foot in their fields, was promoted by Pythagoras, who had likely suffered at least one daylong bout of dizziness, nausea, headaches, and chill from the bean trauma now known as favism. Perhaps someone else in his family had fared far worse. Often, children will go on a binge of eating green fava beans straight from the field, craving fresh foods by the time the harvest comes along. Unfortunately, boys are particularly susceptible to favism because of their limited tolerance for the vicine in the beans. They immediately begin to suffer intense anemia, jaundice, red and black urine, and can succumb to death after two to six days of toxic shock. In Sardinia today, two out of every fifty male children brought to the hospital after consuming favas die from the toxicity.

It may seem odd that Italians have kept eating fava beans while being warned for twenty-two centuries that this food has potentially toxic consequences for them. But up until recently, there have been some missing links in the medical understanding of favism; once put into perspective, the Italian predilection for beans is not irrational at all but supremely adaptive.

Within the last two decades, it has been discovered that the Mediterranean populations' enzyme deficiency that provides resistance to malaria is *enhanced* when traditionally prepared fava beans are regularly consumed, for they contain strong oxidizing agents that rob malaria parasites of the oxygen they need for growth. Women carrying these genes for resistance can eat all the favas they want without suffering anemia, and their resistance to malaria is enhanced by doing so. And as long as men eat dried favas that have been well cooked or consume very low quantities of fresh ones, they too may be given a measure of added resistance to malaria.

The implications of this symbiosis between a traditional food plant and a malaria-exposed human population are staggering, as I later learned from Dr. Solomon Katz, a medical anthropologist from Pennsylvania. Dr. Katz, who has devoted two decades of his lifework to this story, thumped the table where we were sitting as he explained how this is the first good case for the coevolution of genes and culture: "Here is a gene that requires the consumption of a traditional food to confer genetic resistance to a major disease. And unless your culture knows how to prepare the beans to lower their toxic effects, the gene is not adaptive, but deleterious."

Despite occasional deaths to children who have not learned the cultural rules for eating favas, the increased resistance they offer to the entire ethnic population has encouraged their continued consumption. A few years ago, Katz was cautiously optimistic about the evolutionary significance of favas in triggering genetic resistance to malaria; he wrote that "if this hypothesis is fully substantiated, it would provide the first evidence that the biological and cultural evolutions of disease resistance are linked through dietary practices."

Since then, his hypothesis has been confirmed *in vitro* by Israeli researchers; when fava bean substances enter red blood cells infected with malaria parasites, cells lacking the G6PD enzyme do not provide the parasites with enough oxygen, and they die. Italian genes have clearly adapted to the presence of malaria and fava beans. The persistence of favas in their diet suggests values that neither an economist nor a Pythagorean rationalist could ever have predicted.

Mangia-fagioli: the bean eaters. While sampling the Gubbio markets, I had come upon a dozen other kinds of beans being sold—snap beans, chick-peas, cowpeas, and so on—and they were sold by the bagload. Coming from a desert land where local Indians were also called "the bean eaters" in a pejorative way by their neighbors, I realized that few people brag about how many beans they eat. Yet in American deserts as well, native beans protected ethnic groups from the nutrition-related disease to which they were most susceptible: diabetes. Prior to 1920, hardly any desert Indians suffered from adult-onset diabetes. Today nearly half of my Indian neighbors over the age of thirty-five suffer from this "disease of Western civilization."

Over the last five years, I have worked with nutritionists to figure out just why this susceptibility was never expressed when desert Indians were on their traditional diet. We discovered that the beans that formerly dominated their cuisine are among the most effective "slow-release" foods known to humankind. The high-soluble fiber and gum content of desert legumes effectively slow down the digestion of starchy foods and the absorption of resulting sugars into the bloodstream, keeping those people susceptible to diabetes from suffering high blood-sugar levels and pancreatic stress. The historic diet of desert Indians was roughly four times higher in dietary fiber than what their descendants obtain today, and six times richer in fiber than the average American diet. Yet until recently, diabetic Indians were often told to "keep off the beans" by doctors skeptical that any native food could be more nutritious than commercially processed foodstuffs.

Fortunately, many desert Indians continued to eat native beans as well as the favas, peas, and chick-peas introduced from the Old World. These legumes fit well with their dietary preferences and with the desert cropping cycle.

In turn, the availability of green beans from the Americas has reduced the Italian consumption of immature favas straight from the fields, so that fewer now suffer from favism. In a sense, both sets of cultures—desert Indian and Mediterranean—were preadapted to legume consumption and readily incorporated beans from other continents into their diets. Nevertheless, the New World beans do not confer resistance to malaria upon Italians, nor is the present level of consumption of Old World legumes enough to keep Native Americans from developing adult-onset diabetes.

It strikes me as odd that it has taken science so long to confirm that different ethnic groups have metabolically adapted to the mainstays of their traditional diets. Ancel Keys, the nutritional researcher who first proposed that foods that increased blood cholesterol levels were a major causative agent for heart disease, now lives on a Mediterranean diet rich in cholesterol-lowering beans, pasta, salad greens, and monounsaturated olive oil, all washed down with modest quantities of red wine. This, he claims, is among the most nutritious diets that have ever evolved, and it is far more healthful than the K-rations he invented in 1941, just in time for them to pass through sixteen million GI tracts over the following decade. At least the Mediterranean diet appears most nutritious and delicious to those of Mediterranean heritage.

Italian food still does not fit the bill for everyone, or at least not for members of an Apache Indian delegation that recently visited the Vatican. Ecologist Peter Warshall, who accompanied the band of Apache activists, was surprised that they complained of Italian food from the time they left their desert homeland until the time they returned. They became sicker and sicker of it as their Italian hosts tried to outdo one another with more and more authentically Italian recipes. A little venison, some acorn stew, and roasted mescal would have gone a long way toward making those Apaches happy on their Italian holiday.

All this reflection on food traditions made me nostalgic for the Lebanese cuisine that had nurtured me: hummus from chick-peas, taboulch salad, lentils, favas, and stuffed grape leaves. I longed to participate in those traditions again, through gardening and gathering wild plants, particularly the foods that complemented my own genes.

I remembered with some pain the last month that I had lived among the Nabhan clan. I was moving out of a summer cabin on a sand dune above the house where I was born, when I noticed an old friend of my deceased grandfather out on the hillside picking something. I shouted a greeting to Uncle Myron, but he was at least eighty-five by then and couldn't hear me. I heard him, though: he was counting: "Seven thousand eight hundred ninety . . . ninety-one, god-damn it, they're sticking together . . . there, ninety-two, ninety-three . . ."

"What are you counting, Uncle Myron?"

"All the wild grape leaves I've picked for the ladies this summer. They're not as big and tender as the ones in the vineyards in the old country, and some of those ladies bitch at me when I offer them some, as if I'm responsible for how small they are. But at least I've done my share."

I stayed and worked with him for a while, silently.

After a while, Myron turned to me, turned up his hearing aid, and asked, "Gary Paul, after I die, will you make sure those old ladies still get their grape leaves?"

When Uncle Myron asked me to carry on the tradition, I was speechless. After I moved away from home and he had died, I felt like I had failed him as well as members of my family by not being available to continue their customs. I unconsciously endeavored to make up for it by honoring traditional food traditions in other ways and in other places. I have gone from being a cross-cultural seed and fruit trader, like my grandfather Papa John Nabhan, to a promoter of continuing food traditions, like Uncle Myron. Rather than carrying seeds back and forth from one culture to the next, I have become involved in learning how the foods these seeds produce are most valuable *in place*—in the soils, climates, habitats, and cultures where they have evolved the longest.

It has taken me years to realize that cultural continuity is a much more subtle sensibility than what I originally imagined it to be. Although I did not become the provider of leaves to the women in the dunes after Uncle Myron died, I still do harvest grape leaves and cook with them. Although I do not grow Lebanese family heirlooms of favas and lentils and chick-peas, the value of something as simple as a bean has stuck with me. It may take the rest of my life to understand whether I have truly honored what Papa John Nab-han and Uncle Myron have passed on to me.

As Ginger and I came over the mountains from Valdichiasco and into Valfabricca, we purchased some *lupini* and fava beans cured in brine and sat for a moment, munching them, on the edge of the plaza. It was a *piazza centrale* that still func-tioned to link local residents together, especially the old-timers. There, they swapped stories and lies, laughing and arguing with one another, each of them part preacher, part politician, part librarian of local facts.

They must have spotted Ginger and me immediately when we entered the plaza, for after we went into a small grocery store and came out, disoriented, one of them yelled, "Over here!" There, on the corner of the plaza by the main cross street, stood seven old-timers with their canes, potbellies, gestures, and stories. I went up to the closest one and asked him for directions to the official Strada Francescana.

"We're pilgrims. Which is the way that pilgrims have taken when walking to Assisi?"

Before my contact could answer, arms shot out, pointing in every direction. Seven different answers came at once out of seven different mouths, and as they heard each other's recommended directions, their faces filled with color and expression.

"What do you mean, turn left at the next street? The bridge on that street has been closed down for months now!"

Disgusted, another man waved them all off, grabbed Ginger and me by the shoulders, and marched us out into the middle of the main street, where he hobbled along with us until we arrived at the lane where he wanted us to turn. He patted me on the back and grumbled, "There it is, my friends, now go, before the others try to change your minds."

I looked back at his six cronies, and they were still arguing, waving their arms, shaking their canes, and making dramatic gestures to one another with their hands. I had to laugh; we had asked them too large and weighty a question for an afternoon in the week before the Festa di San Francesco: "What is the true Franciscan Way?"

While they argued over the answer, we struck out for the mountaintop village of Pieve di Nicola. Three hours later—after passing vineyards, olive groves, and flocks of hooded crows—we began the long descent into Assisi. Nine and a half hours after starting out that morning, we dropped our packs from our backs on a small lane below the basilica where Saint Francis was buried. In my dreams that night, old men passionately argued with one another: "Which is the way? Which is the way?"

Interlude 6
Vendemmia:
Bringing in the Vintage

rom Valfabricca, the massive range that includes Pieve di Nicola, Monte Subasio, and Monte di Croci, was the only barrier between us and our destination of Assisi. We tried several footpaths that we presumed were parallel to the paved Strada Francescana, but each time we departed for more than a quarter of a mile from the pavement, we dead-ended in someone's ridge-top grain field. We reluctantly returned to the

paved way, for it was already three in the afternoon; we had miles to go before we slept, most of them uphill.

There were cyclones of blackbirds swirling and piles of pumpkins on the roofs of barns as we reached the road's summit. From Monte di Croci down to Assisi, we did little talking; the endorphins killing the pain in our calves and feet numbed our tired bodies. We hobbled the last four miles down to Assisi in the dark, and at the junction of highways below the cathedral, began to ask for directions to the country lodge where we would stay. One driver finally looked at both of us tired souls, shook his head, and said, "Get in—I'll take you there."

It is no overstatement to claim that we were immediately asleep as soon as we put our packs down, took our shoes off, and lay down on our beds. We were much too exhausted after nine days of hiking to muster the strength to absorb all of Assisi's grandeur.

For two days, we recuperated on a small farm at Capodaqua, above the valleys southeast of Assisi in the Subasio foothills. We watched birds, washed clothes, and drank wine from the farm's vineyard; we were still shy about rushing over to Assisi and plunging into its heart, because we had arrived a few days prior to the Feast of Saint Francis. We wanted to see it in full dress, not in its bathrobe as it readied itself for the feast. We would wait for the appropriate moment to dance down its streets.

In the meantime, I arranged for a reprieve. In the days before the feast, Ginger would catch up on other interests, while I would go to the ancient village of Sacrofano an hour from

Rome, to help my friends Pepé Esquinas and Rosanna Galvani with the *vendemmia*, the bringing in of the vintage, and the initiation of wine making in a cave below both their houses, a wine cellar that had not been used for more than thirty years.

The morning of the harvest, Pepé was ill, so Rosanna and I left around seven to drive to some vineyards near Monte Pocchio. She had arranged for us to pick white grapes at a friend's vineyard, under the inspection of an uncle who lived there. We were to work six long rolling rows of grapes that had turned from pale green to blush, most of them already at or slightly past the peak of ripening. Insects, molds, and fungal growths were everywhere. As Rosanna and I began to select only those bunches that had not been burst by juice-sucking insects and covered with a woolly coat of microbes, the old uncle protested, "Take all of them, goddamn it! Don't leave the row half-picked! How are we supposed to make any money off you if we charge you by the amount you pick but you leave the rows in such a mess? No one else will want to glean from your *half-picked* rows, so how will we profit? Anyway, how do you expect to make a full-bodied wine if you don't have some bugs and molds adding to the flavor? I tell you, the little crap that falls into the vats is what gives wine its taste!"

As we reluctantly began to take all the grapes, spoiled and unspoiled, the juices from the grapes already burst by bees and wasps dripped down our hands and arms. We became more and more sticky so that the insects began to swarm all over us, not biting but feeding on the sweet syrups drying on our limbs. I counted a dozen different kinds of insects, present in unbelievable numbers, hovering around

the bunches of grapes, our vats, and our bodies. The *vendemmia*
was not just a significant harvest event for humans but a
ceremony for the attendant fauna as well.

Rosanna and I worked opposite sides of a row, talking
to each other in a mix of Italian and Spanish. We shared
family histories, jokes, and favorite stories about Pepé Esquinas, our mutual friend. In no time, we had picked six
fifty-gallon drums full of grapes and stems, and insects catch-
ing rides with them. I remembered David Price's observation
that true culture is transmitted through stories told during
times of collective labor by hand and "testifies to the survival
of the ancient world . . . binding vines, cutting the olives,
chopping bamboo with handsaws and axes—these are aspects
of a traditional knowledge unsurpassed . . . [by that which
rides on] borrowed or half-owned tractors. And these skills
are still a family patronage." As long as communal work
parties are needed, the stories that reinforce the values of
the community are needed just as much.

Rosanna and I drove back to Sacrofano, where her family
and neighbors helped us roll the barrels of grapes up the
narrow cobblestone walkways in their village. We washed
out other wooden vats, cleaned out the cavern that served
as the wine cellar, crushed the grapes through a hand-cranked
masher, removed the stems from the juice and pulp, and
mixed the batches of juice into other barrels. We found
ourselves stained and sticky up to our armpits; tired, we
returned to her house, where her family had a six-course
meal ready for us. We cleaned up, then sank into our seats
as Pepé poured us some wine, and the family toasted our
work. Then, four of them burst into story simultaneously,
telling of the last times *they* had participated in the *vendemmia*.

I sighed with pleasure as they spoke, for I felt as though I were landing after a long flight away from *family*. I finally had the sense that I had arrived in an Italian community, for I had worked with the grapes and vats and grinders long enough that day to have my outsider's status suspended for the moment. My contribution to their communal work had broken down any notions they may have had about me as a "typical" foreigner on holiday. Now, it seemed, I was considered worthy of hearing their oral histories.

Their stories led out from the ancient wine cellar—a cavern hidden deep beneath their village—through the cobblestone passageways that connected home after home into neighborhood and down through the lineages of wine drinkers who had worked the vats in the cellar, before the wars and after. Their stories moved from favorite vintages and wine makers out into the vineyards that surrounded the village, rising onto the best locations for grape growing and dipping into the ones that they had to fall back on, brushing through the good years and the bad, suffering and yet enduring all the freezes and the plagues and the droughts that they could remember, if not through their own experience, then through the tales of their elders. Their stories noted when certain wine varieties had first come within their range, but they also marked the times when certain families had come and gone, when each had had its heyday, its vintage years, and what had become of its legacy. At first, I thought these were stories about just grapes, but then they were transformed into wine by those crafty alchemists culture and time, and the wine had passed into the bodies of my hosts and become their flesh and the flesh of their neighbors with whom they had shared each batch; and that amalgam of neighbors, who

had first come together by happenstance or by hidden ne-
cessity, had somehow turned into community; and that community had flowed out of the ancient stone homes, back onto
the land, where it began.

We finished off the last of the freshly baked bread and
the last of one bottle of wine and moved from the table to
the sofas and chairs where more wine was poured and more
stories told. Here, I thought, here in the sharing of bread
and wine and story, was where history had its deepest roots.
I could not imagine how the winds of change could ever
topple such a community.

Chapter 7

In September, the season's opening fills the air around here with the noise of early morning warfare, consistent, clumsy shouts of men at badly trained dogs, perhaps an injury, and often not much to show. The development of the hunt . . . has provoked a natural crisis in the animal kingdom, and in that of birds particularly. Some locals are asking whether . . . reserves can remain part of the landscape, and [game can remain in] the kitchen landscape, without more controls.

DAVID PRICE

Feasting on Saint Francis:
Animal Rights and the
Forgotten Forest of Assisi

he morning of October 3, the day before the Feast of Saint Francis, I woke up early and, before coffee, strolled around the farm at Capodaqua, field glasses in hand, hoping to identify the birds whose calls I had heard outside my bedroom window. Coming on an old orchard, I followed some sparrows from tree to tree, without much luck in glimpsing their characteristic markings. After nearly giving up twice,

I finally found a flock in a conifer planted in a windbreak on the edge of the orchard. Just as I was bringing the binoculars into focus, I heard gunfire nearby, and the sparrows were suddenly gone.

I looked around the orchard, and there on the other side of it, a man in jeans and a brown jacket leaned up against his weapon and waved at me.

"Don't you worry. I wasn't shooting at you. I was shooting the other way. Excuse me for scaring you."

I walked back to our rooms at the farmhouse, where Ginger was up and serving herself some coffee.

"How has your morning been? You must have gone outside early." Ginger offered to pour me some coffee.

"Hunters. They've been on our trail since we first climbed La Verna. Not that I think they should stop hunting until we go away. I just get startled, because I don't know where or when to expect them."

"They probably don't know when to expect you either; you're kind of like a seasonal migrant accidentally blown off course, remember?"

"Well, at least we're close to our immediate destination. Let's plan a full day in Assisi." I accepted the coffee cup from Ginger, and we sat down to map out an itinerary for that day, as well as for the festival on the following one.

I had unconsciously built my expectations for these days on the assumption that they would somehow have the tranquillity of my first stay in Assisi a year and a half before. When I had stepped off the train for that initial visit during the height of spring in 1989, I had not been able to speak for an entire day. Anything I might have said would have been drowned out by the songs of multitudinous birds at the peak of breeding season.

Thanks to finches and pigeons hovering over the rose-colored walls of the fortresslike village and to the prenuptial skylarks doing aerial ballets atop Monte Subasio, birdsong had never been out of hearing range. I marveled at how the builders of Assisi's pink and gray stone walls had left open niches and chinks in the masonry as nest holes and perches. I saw little children and old, black-dressed widows broad-casting seeds for the pigeons in the plazas. I watched hooded crows congregate among the ancient olive trees, roosting on moss-covered trunks, and I was delighted when a dozen sparrows bustled out from the conical canopy of a tall Italian cypress. I walked in aural ecstasy from the Little Portion below Assisi to San Damiano—the chapel once restored by Francis himself—to the mountain hermitage of Carceri where tamed white "doves of peace" still flock on the tree where Francis once spoke to them. My immediate conviction was that birds were still a vivid part of the Franciscan terrain.

What I did not see and could not have recognized at the time was that the birds remaining around Assisi lived and died in the midst of a battlefield. The battle pits locals against a conservation campaign of foreign origin, which they feel has been asking Assisi to "take this nature worship too far." For some residents in the Commune of Assisi, the struggle is over whether or not they have the right to hunt in the manner to which they have been accustomed, even if it appalls tourists. For others, it is an issue of Assisi's international reputation being tarnished because hunting and habitat loss have continued for too long on a mountain considered sacred by both Italians and foreigners.

By some accounts, the battle began in the days preceding the Feast of Saint Francis in 1982, when Californian Bert Schwarzchild ascended Monte Subasio on the suggestion of his Swiss friend, conservationist Marissa Cohen. "When I first climbed the mountain," Bert told me in 1990, as we sat in his living room not far from San Francisco Bay, "I knew little about Saint Francis and his relationship with birds. All I knew was that he was loving and caring toward nature. But there I was, on *his* mountain, and everywhere I walked I saw nothing but cartridges and feathers. I didn't see one bird the entire day."

That night, while camping at three thousand feet, not too far down from the cold, exposed summit of Monte Subasio, Schwarzchild could not sleep. He remembered hearing the plaintive call of only one bird the entire night and, while admitting that he is no ornithologist, he guessed it might have been a nightingale. When he descended into Assisi and realized that the town was gearing up to celebrate the eight-hundredth birthday of Saint Francis, he felt obliged to comment to local residents about this irony. He wondered how anyone could justify killing songbirds in the shadow of a place commemorating the patron saint of ecology. A priest with whom he spoke was also concerned about the hunting but was resigned to the notion that a "rest" on the Feast of Saint Francis was all that the hunters would accept. Others were more pessimistic. One woman from Florence told him that she had even seen the hunters shooting at butterflies. Anything that moved seemed to be fair game to some.

Unfortunately for Umbrian hunters, Schwarzchild was not your typical American traveler. A retired engineer and ardent organizer for conservation and human rights, Bert hatched the Assisi Bird Campaign out of what he calls his "contemplative rage." Within a few months of his return to the United States, Schwarzchild walked into the editor's office of *Audubon* magazine and convinced him to publish immediately his report "No Birds Sing on Saint Francis's Mountain." Mere days after its release, the mayor of Assisi began to receive mail by the cartload and wheelbarrow, pleading for a ban on hunting.

No one had a good inventory of bird diversity and abundance on Monte Subasio at the time, but Bert felt sure from his brief visits that "songbirds had been virtually hunted out of the area. Even at the Eremo delle Carceri monastery where Francis had preached to the birds, they had to import trained doves that would stay close to the buildings. The visitors loved to see them on the old oak tree there, but in reality, there were no birds at all, once you got more than a thousand feet away from the place. We decided to bring Saint Francis's birds back to Assisi."

Soon conservationists across Europe joined with Schwarzchild and Marissa Cohen, his friend from the International Union for Conservation of Nature and Natural Resources. They used the crisis in Assisi to focus attention on a larger problem, projecting that as many as 200 million songbirds were being killed each year, while nesting or migrating through Italy, at the hands of a million and a half hunters. The issue had jumped from the glossy pages of *Audubon* and its Italian version, *Uccelli*—where outcry over such matters was expected—to land in *Airone* magazine of Milan, the *Corriere dell'Umbria* of Perugia, and worldwide editions of the *Christian Science Monitor*. Soon, statements of support had been received from Alfredo Biondi, Italy's first minister of ecology, and from Prince Philip, who had been the spearhead for the World Wildlife Fund's 1982 efforts to bring to Assisi leaders from the five major religions of the world in a rallying of ecumenical support for conservation. Others began the long process of lobbying the church to gain its blessings for the birds.

Schwarzchild and his allies seized the time, the place. They organized a September 1983 meeting of conservationists in Assisi, an event that local businesspeople knew might make or break the image of their city as an environmental mecca. It was an image that they did not want undermined. The event would be intensively covered by the press, for it featured the music of New Age composer Paul Winter, the poetry of Italian American Lawrence Ferlinghetti, and the signing of the Declaration of Monte Subasio. Environmentalists would call for a ban on hunting, for the designation of a regional park and world cultural heritage site, and for the establishment of an international center for environmental education and ethics. The antihunting lobby would gain considerable momentum through all the free publicity.

Hoping at least to generate a consensus in support of the park, Mayor Gianfranco Costa consented to host an environmental discussion at city hall. But word got around that there would be a debate on whether or not to ban hunting immediately, and Mayor Costa soon began to receive death threats. Local hunters were not so keen on revenues from ecotourism that they were willing to toss in their guns and khakis without a fight. And they argued that the international protectionists' antihunting campaign had a strong anti-Italian feeling embedded in it; as *Airone*'s editor feared, this prejudice might spread.

It is true that Italian hunters had been categorically criticized by American and northern European environmentalists many times in the past, for they had continued to shoot eleven species of birds and mammals that were by then fully protected in other European countries. Now, however, there was dismay among rural Italians that their "green" urban kin were playing into the hands of foreigners. Earlier in the century, a similar battle had taken place in New York City, when American zoologist William Hornaday had called Italian immigrants "guerrillas of destruction who shot our most useful and sweet songsters" for the dinner pail. Hornaday and his elitist cohorts in the Boone and Crockett Club were not so much against sport hunting as they were worried that this gentlemanly pursuit might "degenerate, as it has in Italy, to the popping of robins, sparrows, and bobolinks."

Although none of Schwarzchild's statements had the racist overtones of Hornaday's, any attack on the Umbrian hunting tradition could bring out a certain paranoia in Umbrians. They were even sensitive to criticism from other Italians, for the percentage of the Umbrian population that hunts is three times the national average and the highest of any provincial population in Italy. Their hunters' associations had been taking a defensive posture for years, glibly dismissing any suggestion that their sport produced ecological impacts. Umbrian hunters testily asserted that "more birds are killed in the United Kingdom and Germany by domestic cats than by hunters in Italy."

As the "bird day" arrived in Assisi, the streets were filled with tension. Doves were symbolically released into the air, and music floated through the streets, but the event scheduled for city hall looked as though it might become volatile. The hall filled early, and city fathers appeared worried over the wording of the declaration, for it mandated a permanent, year-round ban on hunting birds on the whole of Monte Subasio and in the entire territory of the Commune of Assisi. Not long after the discussion began, however, the door of city hall was flung open, and a large delegation of the four Franciscan "families" appeared. With them was His Eminence Cardinal Silvio Oddi and his environmental liaison. The hall fell quiet.

"Where is this declaration I want to sign?"

Not another word needed to be said.

With the cardinal's support for the moratorium made obvious, few Italians would speak out against his concerns. It had taken months of lobbying with church bureaucrats to convince them to take a stand, but once the cardinal spoke, the formal debate ended.

In recounting this story to me, Schwarzchild beamed with delight. "I had finally come to realize why the Catholic church considers itself to be eternal. It takes an eternity to get the church to respond!"

Since September 1983, the Umbrian government has been responding with *Divieto di Caccia* signs that prohibit hunting on Monte Subasio. Hundreds of such signs have been nailed up on trees along Subasio's trails and roadways. When I asked local hunters about them, most of them claimed, as Romano Bazzoffia did, that the ban does not affect them: "In the woods of Monte Subasio, there hasn't been any real hunting since the days of my father."

Sportsmen in the Assisi vicinity insist that their interest

in hunting has favored the presence of animals through pro-motion of measures to protect and improve forest habitats. A few maintain that the moratorium only applies to hunting on public lands during the Feast of Saint Francis itself. Others bitterly complain that they can no longer carry their rifles onto the mountain at any time without fear of punishment.

I saw a number of No Hunting signs with bullet holes shot through them. Since there is only one game warden for every nine hundred Umbrian hunters on the land, law en-forcement officers hardly affect poaching or overhunting at all.

The day before the Feast of Saint Francis, two gun-toting hunters and their dogs trailed down Subasio's slopes while I was climbing toward the hermitage.

"Any luck?" I asked hesitantly.

"Not any *good* luck today," one hunter replied, looking at his sidekick. "I don't know if my partner here brings me the bad luck or if it is his dog!"

They both laughed and continued down the slopes toward Assisi, giving no indication that they felt any need to be discreet about hunting on the mountain. Other rounds of fire echoed over the Umbrian plain. The men whose paths I'd crossed were not alone in their casual disregard of the moratorium.

When I went into a bar not far from Assisi to use the phone, two old-timers, half-crocked, took me under their wings. They bought me a glass of local red wine, then another, and encouraged me to take a look around at the memorabilia on the walls from their hunting club, "The Society of the Frying Pan."

One of their club members was a superb cartoonist, and

conservationists had become the favorite butt of his jokes. One of his masterworks showed wary wildlife ducking the shots of hunters so that the bullets sailed past them to hit protectionist "spies" hiding behind trees. Another cartoon was in the form of a dinner invitation: "The Society for the Protection of Animals and the World Wildlife Fund are invited to be the honored guests of the Frying Pan Society at a dinner featuring pigeons, starlings, larks, sparrows, crows, and wagtails, newly initiated to the frying pan by our beloved founders."

If Umbrian hunters were all able to catch their bag limits, 124 million birds and mammals would be taken out of forests and off farmlands. Some of those captured or killed would be birds that preferentially nest around fields and hedges—species adapted to the cultural landscapes of Italy. But Umbrian law also permits the killing of nineteen threatened migratory species and ten other internationally protected birds. There is no doubt that animal populations remain at risk as long as such permissive and poorly enforced hunting laws prevail in Umbria. Yet the focus on hunting as the primary cause of wildlife depletion in Italy is to some extent a misleading one.

The oldest conservation organization in the world—the International Council for the Preservation of Birds—has recently compiled much of the existing information on songbird declines in Europe. While twenty out of thirty-seven migratory species studied showed marked population decreases, the council's collaborating scientists are hesitant to blame hunting as the major factor triggering the declines. In some cases, the drops in populations appear more strongly related to the disruption of migratory corridors by converting wildlands to mechanized farms, residential areas, or factories. In other instances, birds have been decimated by the chemical contamination of food and water supplies by pollution and pesticides. The declines of some migratory species, such as whitethroats, were explained less by hunting and habitat change in Europe than by the effects of the Sahelian drought on winter food availability in northern Africa.

Like many others, I had earlier been quick to point the finger at hunters as the culprits causing the collapse of bird populations, but I now have more difficulty assessing all the subtle and varied interactions between birds and declining habitat quality. Many of the remaining birds are adapted to farmlands and wood lots, but others cannot be supported without sufficient wildlands along their migration corridors. My guess is that hunting has merely exacerbated the reduction in bird diversity initiated long ago by the insidious degradation and fragmentation of forests and marshlands, trends that continue unabated today.

It is easy for me to see spent cartridges and blasted feathers, but how can I tell if a forest's structure and function have been irreparably degraded? I pondered this dilemma while hiking with Ginger to the Eremo delle Carceri, halfway up Monte Subasio. It was here that both Gianfranco Bologna of the World Wildlife Fund/Italy and Marissa Cohen, another conservationist, said that I would find a contrast to the forest plantations of exotic conifers that now flank much of the mountainside.

"Eremo delle Carceri is the only area on Mount Subasio with some natural forest," offered Gianfranco, "and I believe it is because the Franciscans have always kept it in their hands. Two lovely oaks logged out elsewhere—*Quercus ilex* and *Quercus pubescens*—persist there in dense stands."

"Fortunately, some of the old original tree cover does remain," agreed Marissa. "The woods around the Franciscan hermitage have been left intact from the time when Saint Francis talked to the birds. The whole area is permeated with a magnetic stillness."

But when Ginger and I began to hike in the darkness beneath the giant canopy of the Carceri forest, we found something profoundly disturbing about its stillness. Birds and small mammals scurried around only in low numbers, yet the prevailing silence may have had more to do with the trees themselves than with the possibility that the place had been overhunted. The trees looming large overhead were all about the same size and age; the canopy was closed. I saw sparse understory growth, for little light reached the forest floor. There was a complete absence of gaps opened up by deadfalls and natural snags.

In a time when we are learning that old-growth forest patches are ancient but vital landscapes, I felt reluctant to say aloud what my senses were telling me: this old forest was senescent and in decline. There had been fire suppression and static preservation far too long, and now there was hardly any sign of natural regeneration. The Franciscans had preserved a small patch of natural forest like a sacred icon stashed away for centuries, but it had lost its currency, its dynamism.

As I was sitting in the darkness, lamenting that this notion had even popped into my mind, I noticed something that verified that certain trees were on their way out. Away from the main trail through the Carceri forest, I could see woodpiles hidden from the sight of most visitors. I got up to walk around and count them. Thirty-seven piles of holm oak and other large trees had been neatly stacked, and the girths of the cut trunks were enormous. It was clear that these newly cut trunks had been ravaged by boring insects when the trees were still standing.

A lightning strike or storm damage could hardly account for so much wood needing to be cut in one fell swoop. Had the trees died of old age or of the obvious insect infestation? Would more frequent fires have reduced the insect populations and allowed a mix of trees more varied in age?

I could not divine the forest's biological history, but I could at least tally up its diversity of plant species. During three visits to the forest over two seasons, I tried to collect every species of tree, shrub, wildflower, grass, and fern I could find over the couple dozen acres of forest closest to the hermitage. I took the smallest possible diagnostic part with me to the University of Perugia, where botanists familiar with the local flora assisted me in identifying them.

In all, I tallied a mere seventy species—in the same amount of time, I've collected as many on a single acre at the desert's grassland edge and twice as many on a few acres of desert oasis or tropical forest. Put simply, the Carceri forest is as impoverished as a forest of its type ever gets. This forest is pitifully low in diversity of life forms, as well as being simplified in structure.

The Franciscans have been bent on protecting a few noteworthy trees, but they are close to losing a forest. I was struck by this as Ginger and I walked back to the hermitage itself. Just before we arrived at the buildings, we came to the thousand-year-old tree where Saint Francis had spoken to the birds and they had hushed themselves to hear him. The ancient tree had a trunk split for nearly half its length. Some of its limbs were already dead, and it was teetering on the edge of an eroded gully. To keep it upright and rooted, the tree had been cabled and chained to the stone walls nearby. It was like a terminally ill elderly patient on life-support machines in a hospital: unable to live freely but also unable to go ahead and die, to give the space to someone else. The Franciscans have turned a fabled tree into a decrepit monument and may have forgotten the forest behind it.

While everyone had an opinion regarding the ban on hunting in the Declaration of Monte Subasio, the call for a regional park—a larger area in which remnant wildness would be protected—is less remembered. The park efforts have proceeded slowly, from elaboration of an exhaustive master plan by the University of Perugia through Umbrian provincial government review and approval. It is now up to the Umbrian and Italian governments to do something tangible for Monte Subasio.

Professor Franco Tassi, who has served as director of the Italian Committee for National Parks and Reserves, has been impatient about all of this. "The region of Umbria is particularly late in executing a plan for parks and protected areas." He has called for Umbria to meet "the challenge of 10 percent"—that is, of increasing the amount of land protected from the current 1.5 percent to a full 10 percent.

As Ginger and I walked back down from the Carceri miniforest to Assisi's stone-wall enclosure, I wondered where this other 8.5 percent of wildlands might be found. We passed pastures overgrazed by sheep, limestone quarries, and the straight rows of exotic conifers now called "forests" here.

The answer may be that the forests of Monte Subasio need to be restored in the spirit that Saint Francis demonstrated when he responded to the divine call at the deteriorated chapel of San Damiano: "Francis, can't you see my house falling into ruin? Go, and repair it for me."

Carla Collesi and her colleagues at the Assisi Nature Council are doing just that, by planting native forest species on quarried hills and abandoned pastures on the other side of Monte Subasio. In 1988, as part of a "Peace with Nature" environmental education event, four hundred trees were planted by children and their parents on a scarred slope above a country highway. A few acres of planted nursery stock cannot remake a forest, but if these recent plantings could be followed by a sowing of more of the original Apennine flora, it would move the vegetation in the right direction.

The International Children's Grove is only one of several restoration projects planned by the council. The trees were still knee to waist high when Ginger and I walked around the grove in late afternoon, after leaving the Carceri hermitage. Before I left, I dropped onto my knees and peeked through their foliage down toward Assisi. Through needles and leaves, I watched a pale lemon sun slide behind the clouds above the castlelike Rocca Maggiore. It was fitting to see the ancient village shrouded in green again. We stayed in the grove until dark, then descended on Assisi in the midst of the feast.

A fleet of dark clouds hung low over the town and the slopes of Subasio by the time Ginger and I returned within the stone walls. A full moon rolled in and out of sight as the clouds continued their stormy march. Down in the Basilica di San Francesco, brown-robed brothers were finishing their solemn celebration of Transitus, the passing of Saint Francis from this world. I had tried to enter the basilica earlier in the day, but there were too many activities going on, too many people. I had felt ill inside, detached from what had brought me here.

I could not bring myself to crowd into a darkened room with thousands of others to celebrate the life of a man who had so desperately struggled to stay *outside*—outside the walls of cities and monasteries, outside the traps of static, institutionalized religion. So I let slip by my chance to be in on the ecclesiastical formalities meant to honor my saint. I had come two hundred miles on foot to celebrate this day but had backed off from sitting at his crowded table; we had been on his mountain instead.

As the Transitus mass ended, hundreds of brown-robed Franciscans poured out onto the plaza. I could see how the experience had deeply moved many of the brothers who had been in the cathedral. As they came outside, the bells tolled in a low rumble for nearly fifteen minutes. I finally had to look up to the sky, the rumble reminded me so much of the thunder that marks the coming of a storm.

I saw no lightning, but I did see a rim of light as haunting as anything I have ever seen. All along the perimeter of the village, tens of thousands of torchlike fires were lit atop the stone walls and towers, clear to the far reaches of Porta San Giacomo and Rocca Maggiore. Coca-Cola and Peroni beer cans had been cut in half, filled with oil and a wick, and lighted. I heard someone say that the oil was a gift from the

Venetians, who were cohosting the feast this year. I asked a local cab driver about the lights of burning oil.

"What is the oil that they are burning in the votive lamps?"

"*Oil*. What do you mean, what kind of oil? When we say *oil*, we mean *olive oil*. If it's another kind of oil, well, we say that: *motor* oil, *sunflower* oil, you know?"

"So it was olive oil that the Venetians brought as a gift to Assisi?"

"Well, they bring just a little of it from their homeland. Let's say it's *symbolic*. The real oil they bring with them is *this* . . ." He rubbed imaginary cash between his fingers. "But the Venetians, they did not bring too many of themselves to Assisi to cohost the *festa*. I know, because I am a taxi driver, so my meter measures the size of the *feast*. Perhaps five hundred came from Venice this year, and they will only stay two days, then head back to work. Venetians don't live by the saints, they live by business. Other people, though, they still remain close to the saints. When it was Sicily's turn to give the oil, twenty thousand Sicilians arrived and they spent a week dancing in the streets."

He was right about the tone of this year's events; they had a businesslike undercurrent. The only dancing was by a staged folk group in costume, from Venezia e Gualdi. The crowd hardly responded to them. Well-dressed families slowly proceeded up the streets to have a quiet meal in one of the restaurants. Ginger and I were going to scan a few of the menus, then decide on a place for a light meal, but my first menu reading stopped me dead in my tracks.

"Featured tonight are delicious cannelloni, served with filet al Rubesco, or pigeon cooked Assisi-style . . ."

. . .

On the morning of the Feast of Saint Francis, we arrived in town late from Capodaqua. The festivities had already begun. Minstrels in medieval garb were wandering the streets, playing flutes, piccolos, and lutes. We saw them moving toward the Piazza del Commune and followed them to where a large crowd was assembling. Soon our attention was turned to a veiled object in the middle of the plaza where political dignitaries, media celebrities, and a few religious luminaries had gathered.

Suddenly a bald dwarf in a green suit moved in front of these guests of honor and splashed a bucketful of wheat seed onto the plaza's cobblestones at their feet. Immediately, thousands on thousands of domestic pigeons and doves descended from the tops of the Templo di Minerva and surrounding palazzos, blurring the scene with the frenzied beating of their wings. While the birds dove down to feed on the grain, the dignitaries whisked away the huge white sheet, unveiling a Statue of Liberty. Or sort of. It was an ungodly plaster-of-paris statue of a cartoon Felix the Cat, holding the torch of freedom!

The excited birds flew in every direction, but none landed on the cat. A banner rose above it, proclaiming "Cruelty-Free Animal Liberation." Representatives from the Green Federation of Italy and the Assisi Natural Council invited everyone to attend their full-day conference on animal rights and to purchase products from their exposition of health and beauty aids developed without the use of animal testing.

That was not all. A pickup truck belonging to Radio Hare Krishna Central arrived with a remote recording studio tucked into its camper trailer and did on-the-spot interviews with an emaciated Italian Hare Krishna leader and a large, bearded rabbi in a full gray robe and red felt *yarmulke*. The Hare Krishnas had apparently walked from Florence to Assisi, accompanied by carts drawn by water buffaloes and full of gurus and gear, as well as by their mobile recording studio. I was surprised and relieved to learn that they had hiked roughly the same route as we had, but a couple of days later.

I looked around for Franciscans in the plaza but didn't see any at first. There were, however, many other characters to see. Standing next to Ginger was a European version of Dolly Parton, a bleached blonde in her early fifties wearing a country-style print dress and carrying two homemade handbags. I guessed that they were homemade because they were the only cloth bags I've ever seen that had little windows on the sides. I looked closer and saw that each bag carried a toy poodle, which was looking out its window at the buffalo-drawn cart that had just arrived with a deeply meditative guru inside.

Dolly became extremely excited and pulled a miniature camera out of the bosom of her dress. She snatched one of the poodles out of its bag, hugged it, and then placed it a few feet in front of the water buffaloes, the cart, and the guru. When the poodle turned its head toward her, she snapped its picture, then swept it up and put it back in the bag.

I was reminded of the words of ecologist Paul Shepard, who has argued that animals lose their *otherness* when brought across the domestic threshold and dressed, bagged, or harnessed: "What can be the existential status of the institutionalized domestic animals as well as the family dog and cat?" Shepard asked a number of "pet therapists" and environmental ethicists at a small meeting we attended. "They are clearly happy friends of mankind—just see how they wag their tails and purr? . . . [And yet] even schoolkids know that wolves did not *decide* to become dogs. . . . [We have tried to use domestic pets] to represent wild animals in our psychological development and well-being, in those inmost events that make us human. The colossal upsurge of the pet as an industrialized therapeutic agent brings the issue of our inner life before us, as does the world's diminishing *wild* abundance and diversity."

I wondered if the poodle-cuddling matron next to me had ever compared her tail-wagging pet to wolves and its other wild forebears; for her, dogs and wolves were probably apples and oranges. But they are not; we have simply drained most of the wild juices out of pets until they no longer have the same "taste" as their wild ancestors. Animal rights activists who restrict themselves to the issue of welfare for pets have failed to confront root causes: for hundreds if not thousands of years, certain societies have cruelly bred dogs for the ultimate make-over, so that they now resemble us more than they do wolves. Our pets can purr, cuddle, and wag their coiffured tails, but they can hardly feed themselves anymore, and this transmutation was not of their own choosing.

To me, Shepard's words are a critique not so much of our pets but of our society as a whole in its quest to domesticate, tame, and institutionalize anything it finds that is wild, threatening, or beyond human control. Thus, organized religion is perhaps simply tamed spirituality—a spirituality that seldom speaks to the wild side of our souls. Surely, in diminishing the wild world around us, we have diminished the wild spirit within us as well.

By this time, the Hare Krishnas were chanting and dancing, undulating between the cart and the plaster cat. A crowd of young antivivisectionists and animal rights activists gathered to watch. One woman wore a Greenpeace T-shirt, which bore the slogan "Your Mother Is in Danger" across her breasts. An antivivisectionist served as a beast of burden for a pair of wooden signs, one in front and one behind her, advertising New Age cosmetics: "Born of the Green Earth, Without a Trace of Animal Flesh" and "Keep Animal Experimentation out of My Makeup!"

I then saw that a plaza storekeeper was arguing with one of the Krishna brothers, who had asked for the intervention of a police officer. The storekeeper kept on waving his hands, then pointing down at a big pile of water buffalo dung that had been dropped right in front of the entrance to his grocery. He was complaining that the customers were accidentally stepping in it and carrying manure into his clean store.

A few clerics had just arrived from the Piazza Sur di San Francesco where the "legitimate celebration" of the feast had taken a break. When they saw the Hare Krishnas jumping up and down singing, "Hare! Hare! Hare!" their expressions changed from puzzlement to annoyance.

My attention then turned to a nun who was being pigeonholed by one of the obviously Italian Hare Krishnas. He was trying to give her a promotional pamphlet for the second time in a matter of minutes.

"No! No! No!" she said, her voice growing shrill. "You

know that this is a solemn day for Catholics, a day to reflect on the life of *our* saint!"

The Hare Krishna backed away. "I'm sorry, sister, but he's everybody's saint now."

By early afternoon, I was deeply tired; nevertheless, I found it easy to stay awake during the infuriating roundtable discussion "San Francesco: Primo Animalista?" It began with a young woman, who introduced the theme by stating, "Eight hundred years since Saint Francis walked this ground, and Assisi still has no animal shelter . . ." I was amazed that she seemed to assume that we could redress our relationship to nature simply by taking better care of the overabundance of pets. While I hoped that my untrained ears were missing certain subtleties of Italian rhetoric, I did hear enough catchphrases to give me the sense that few profundities were shared that afternoon.

One New Age philosopher offered these elucidating remarks: "Francis has always been thought of as strange, even by the Italian people from whom he emerged. Strange, because he was born before the time for his ideas had arrived. He was for peace at a time when everyone in Assisi and Perugia aimed at killing one another. He was for animal rights when everyone was hunting. Well, I want to tell you this: his time has now come."

Compared to the war being raged against wild animals and their habitats all around the world, the focus of an international meeting on a local pet shelter seemed like a gesture of misplaced concern. If treating the world *humanely* has been reduced to efforts to further *humanize* animals, we are headed in the wrong direction. I was beginning to be bothered as much by the notion of building a structure to *house* animals as I was by the parallel notion: that we can house the spirit in a temple, cathedral, or brocaded ox cart.

One of the Italian Hare Krishnas joined the panel to tell how he had turned from Catholicism to Eastern traditions of spirituality, without ever having forgotten Saint Francis: "I just walked from Florence to Assisi to pay homage to Saint Francis, a saint for every species, every religion. The journey has been beautiful, man."

I was deciding whether to go and take a real nap elsewhere, when I caught this sentiment in the very last speech: "Francis is to Italy what Gandhi is to India. He would not eat flesh. He lived off vegetables. Saint Francis felt that animals were like us—his brothers—and that the world would be a better place if animals did not kill one another. This is a feeling I share totally."

To me, this sounded like a message from those who would tame wolves, turn them into vegetarians, and change their remaining wild habitats into "better places," perhaps soybean fields and tofu factories. I had read oodles of texts on Saint Francis, yet had never run across any that demonstrated Francis to be a pure vegetarian. Nor had I come across anything that suggested herbivory as the only holy way for all of the animal kingdom. Would the speaker have gone on to condemn all carnivores and parasites as evil by nature?

I puzzled over the traps and travesties inherent in a worldview where animals are "like us," remade in our own image. We rob them of their distinctiveness, and by doing so, we ultimately diminish the richness of this world. For

that matter, plants are equally diminished by reducing them
to the "only acceptable food," for then *their* "otherness" is
not respected either. Why is it more natural or spiritual to
crush plant tissue against our molars than it is to rip animal
flesh with our incisors? Why uproot plants if they are part
of creation as much as animals are?

I could hear ringing through my ears the words that my
Alaskan friend Richard Nelson had said, distilling the wisdom
he had gained after years of living with Athapaskan and Inuit
hunters: "All of us live by ingesting the lives of others. We
can do this with respect for the plant or animal that will die
so that we can live, or we can do it mindlessly."

Such mindful respect, by its very nature, somehow con-
nects the life of a plant or animal back to its habitat, its roots.
While many of the discussants were bright, compassionate
people, I still felt a certain lack of connection between their
conservation concerns and wild nature, as if animals existed
only as toys, cart drawers, or symbols. The animals of which
they spoke were either pets or abstractions—animals with
no relationship to other creatures or to the wild habitats
where they originated.

I had begun to feel claustrophobic again, as though I too
needed something more than a handbag with a window in
its side in order to feel at home. I was hot and headachy; I
needed to get beyond lecture halls filled with folding chairs,
beyond chapels and basilicas filled with fine art, and beyond
plazas featuring plaster cats to feel the life within myself. I
slipped over to where Ginger was sitting and told her where
I would meet her in a couple of hours.

And so I walked. I walked down the Corso Mazzini and
past the Piazza di Santa Chiara, named for Francesco's beloved

friend, Clare. I despaired when I remembered that some pope has labeled her the matron saint of television. I began to walk faster then, remembering these words from Madge Midley's *Beast and Man*: "Man is not adapted to live in a mirror-lined box, generating his own electric light and sending for selected images from outside when he happens to need them. Darkness and bad smell are all that can come from that. We need a vast world, and it must be a world that does not need us; a world constantly capable of surprising us, a world we did not program, since only such a world is the proper object of wonder."

I was walking briskly now. I escaped from the city, passing out of the Porta Nuova. Descending the hill, I headed for the sanctuary of San Damiano a few blocks away, a place I had once imagined to be far out in the country. I caught my breath in an old olive grove, the ancient gnarled trees having somehow recovered from killing frosts several years back. Then, once at the sanctuary, I couldn't stand either to sit still or to tour the buildings, nor was I ready to leave.

I gradually made my way down to a small, almost hidden terrace of the orchards, below a bridge. It was littered with garbage tossed down from above, Peregrino orange juice cans and Eskimo Pie wrappers. I started to pick up this human litter and put it into a pile, and I spent several minutes retrieving broken glass and rusted metal cans that had found their way into the unruly growth between the bridge and the orchard.

Slowly, my attention turned to the fruit tree cuttings and other wood scraps that I found thrown off to the side of the orchard. I began to build with them.

While mockingbirds and finches sang in the trees above

me, I planted miniature posts upright. Atop forked corner posts, I ran other sticks horizontally, to form the beams of a roof. I piled more sticks from beam to beam and pruned a sprig from a rosebush into the shape of a green cross to plant on the roof. I began to stack sticks alongside the building to make walls, but then I knocked them down. I imagined a church without walls—only doorways—in which no one could close himself or herself off and forget the wildness outside. There would be no floor, except for the soil. I changed my mind about the design and opened up the roof as well, planting the former roof beams farther and farther away from the skeletal structure, turning them into the beginnings of a forest.

"Restore my church?" I mumbled to myself. "Your proper church is the living earth, for it is all hallowed ground." And I vowed never again to focus my worship in a static, lifeless church. My days in apprenticeship with the secular Franciscans were coming to a close, I could feel; now I would move toward more fully apprenticing myself to the flowers and the birds. I had become a pilgrim to seek out my feelings about the wild spirit and the institutions that are built around it; these sooner or later try to contain it, unless they are constantly reopened to the larger world. Francesco di Bernardone loved that wild spirit and felt its presence throughout the natural world. And yet, even he had difficulty keeping his own order focused on nurturing that spirit rather than on building institutions that would cut off the flow of fresh air. We must return to what most fundamentally inspires us; without that breathing space, we will atrophy and die.

. . .

From my "refound" sanctuary, I ran until the slope became too steep and then walked up the main trail toward Eremo delle Carceri outside the Porta Cappuccini. The trail wound through forest plantation, pasture, and quarry, but I was so ignited that I hardly noticed a thing until I had passed through the protected forest of Carceri and reached the other side. I then climbed over an old stone wall, under a fence, and ended up in a truffle reserve where I had seen hunters walking before.

This mosaic of forest and glade was not pristine, but it was not overly managed either. It was younger, more varied than the Carceri forest proper, and richer in flowers. There was light filtering in, not just the heavy shadows of ancient trees; because of that, little plants were not excluded. I loved seeing the waifs—blackberry and verbascum, ginestra and eryngium—mixed with the longer-lived forest dwellers— cypress and oak, fir, pine, and poplar. In one secluded spot off the trail, I found a patch of head-nodding cyclamen in full flower.

"Panporcino!" I cried. I had not seen these little wild- flowers since La Verna. I went down on my belly with them, lying in the midst of a mix of tree litter and dead tufts of grass in order to marvel at a life no larger than the span of my hand. I knew that cyclamens were now found in so few places that they had been protected by Umbrian law. Yet here, where old hunters wander and truffle grubbers dig, a few rarities somehow hung on tenaciously. Here was a flower that linked the wild and the cultured in my mind, that I had

seen in the shrines at the start of our trip in the sacred groves of La Verna and now, at the end, in the waysides of Monte Subasio.

I had come to Italy looking for a fresh dynamic between culture and nature, between tradition and spontaneity, between civility and wildness. I could now feel that dynamic emerging, one in which each of these poles could be respected for what it was without diminishing the other. True culture needs wildness as a reference point—"nature as measure," as Wendell Berry has put it—and that reference point disappears if wildness is so fully co-opted, absorbed, or contained that it loses its essential character.

For the last century, conservationists have endeavored to isolate patches of nature from the reach of human manipulation, to reserve land that is "hands off" to people, where wildness will not be compromised. But over the course of history, as David Quammen has put it, "the object-ground relations have reversed. Wild landscapes survive only as enclaves in a matrix of human dominion. These enclaves are so few, so starkly demarcated, that we label them individually—with names like Yosemite, Bob Marshall, Serengheti, Royal Chitwan, Arctic National Wildlife Refuge." La Verna and Subasio could be among those names.

It may be that we need something else as much as we need these postage-stamp enclaves of so-called pristine nature, because they are now too small and too precious to accommodate everyone's need to touch the wild again. Once the "object-ground relationship" flip-flopped, most people forgot the wildness beyond as well as within themselves. For society to know the ultimate value of such land, perhaps we need other places as *contact zones*—for knowing and healing, for restoring the wild natives and for restoring ourselves.

In other words, we need something more than rigorously protected forests and pristine parklands to keep us whole. We need not dispense with the formalities of parks and refuges, but we must recognize something else that is vital: the essential *forms* of nature, the underlying variety, are more complex than our capability to appreciate or circumscribe, and are fundamental to our welfare. We should turn our attention toward *rough country*, unmanaged and unmapped except in the minds of truffle grubbers and mating larks. We need land where we can be truant and not have to pay to get in or be inspected on the way out. Each of us needs to sneak into country still unvisited by the masses, even if that means waking up at five before most people roll out of bed.

If you cannot find terrain magnificent enough to take your breath away, gravitate to places that can at least increase your heartbeat. Find land fit for the raccoons, foxes, or hares, and if the animal numbers eventually recover, for the occasional hunter to wander through without causing worry —country where you are satisfied by your encounters with other creatures, whether you hunt them or not. Let it have enough of its wildness left for the wildflowers to flourish— those that D. H. Lawrence saw and lauded—but let it be country with more than that as well. It needs to be land that allows the possibility of glimpsing vagrant wolves, untamed truffles, and unexpected migrant birds, land where you sense their presence in your pulse, land where their fragrance catches and lingers on the breeze.

I, for one, will always need to have contact with rough

country, beyond the tamed world of human artifice. If I do not, then vivisection will become more than a fate to protest for what it does to other animals. It will be what I have done to myself. I would rather join the cyclamen and live out my days beyond the stone walls of the city, in the spaces where culture does not overwhelm nature in their dance together.

Epilogue:
Where Did We Go
After the Journey?

fter Ginger and I left Assisi to return to America, I kept hoping that the realizations which emerged over the pilgrimage could somehow be applied to my everyday life. If it was even possible for two weeks of my life to set the course for all the rest, I was unsure of just how these days of dancing down an unfamiliar trail had redirected my entire trajectory. Yet those vivid moments of juxtaposing wildness with culture,

the Mediterranean with the Americas, and tradition with
spontaneous expression became the nursery that stocked the
next two years of my life. The seeds that germinated on
Italian soil have now been rooted into the earth of my daily
life to a depth that I could not have imagined as our pilgrimage
ended.

I have not yet stepped back into a Catholic church for
worship since the time of the pilgrimage, and I remain ambivalent about my relationship to the formal Franciscan tradition. I did end my apprenticeship with the Franciscan priests
and lay brothers, and I did begin one with the birds, the
plants, the lizards, moths, and mammals of my home. I had
studied and written about some of them before, but in ways
that may have inadvertently homogenized some of their distinctive qualities rather than shown full respect by keeping
their otherness inviolate. They have lives separate from our
own emotional impositions on them; they are not simply
"brothers like us." To consider the discreteness of their lives,
to attempt to represent them without romanticizing, com-
promising, or accidentally defiling them is a difficult task but
one toward which I have turned more and more of my
attention.

Yet a Franciscan thread still weaves its way through my
work. My energy has become increasingly focused on the
rarest of the rare in this world: the neglected species and
cultures that our society does not recognize or care about.
Much of my recent research has been devoted to the conservation of the endangered desert biota associated with the
ancient cactus and ironwood forests of northern Mexico.
These resources form the basis of traditional life of the Seri
Indians, one of the last hunter-gatherer groups in North

America, but they have been threatened by charcoal production and rangeland conversion. I am no longer happy with simply collecting rare seeds and the last stories about them; I want to see them remain, evolving, in place. They deserve more than mere survival in a seed bank; they need to have their wild places returned to them so that they may thrive. Were Francesco di Bernardone a biologist today, I'm sure that his care, too, would extend to these creatures.

The Franciscan trail weaves through my life in other ways as well. I have chosen to direct my professional activities through informal networks of friends and small, young grass-roots organizations, rather than through investing all my loyalties in universities or fraternal orders that often fall out of touch with the people they are meant to serve. I am fortunate that I can now do much of my work beyond any office, from my home or in the field. As my friend David Ehrenfeld has written recently, "it is easy to see that loyalty in its original form has survival value. . . . What concerns me is a much more modern loyalty . . . the loyalty to institutions. Should a person be loyal to an organization? I think we run up against a dangerous and self-destructive perversion of the ancient and honorable trait of loyalty . . . by entrusting our wealth, leadership, and environments to immortal organizations; we subject our descendants to a likelihood of poverty, misdirection, and environmental degradation."

It is clear to me that Saint Francis was emotionally crushed by the transformation of his grass-roots gathering of brothers into yet another bureaucracy of the church; I can't imagine that the best way to honor his vision is by feeding that bureaucracy rather than by informally reaching out to the neglected lives around us.

I have also continued to learn about loyalty from my friend Ginger Harmon. She has stayed with me, physically and emotionally, through the pilgrimage and beyond. She has become part of my family, and I, hers.

And two years to the month after our pilgrimage, Ginger "gave Caroline and me away to each other." Having guided us for so long, Ginger was the natural choice for first speaker on our behalf at a sunset ceremony in which Caroline and I became married.

Our wedding did not take place in a church but outside, at a place called Lodge on the Desert, where cactus and creosote bushes surrounded us, with mountains on the horizons. Our minister was not a Catholic priest but an old running partner of mine, the director of the local chapter of the Audubon Society. My children walked with us, carrying a banner that they themselves had colored. Friends and family gathered with us in the celebration, as did wild seeds and garden fruits from the home ground of each visitor. Birds flitted through the trees, welcome but aloof and unconcerned with what we humans were doing that day.

Thus, Caroline and I came before our community and took vows before its members. We did not celebrate a formal communion, but I could not come together with so many loved ones without returning to that ancient, universal ritual: the breaking of bread—in this case, Lebanese pita—and the tasting of wine. I remembered the words of Ignazio Silone: "Bread is made of many grains of corn. . . . Wine is made of many grapes, so it means unity, too. . . ."

At one point in our wedding rite, each friend and kinsman was asked to bring forth seeds that he or she had brought from a garden or the rough country closest to his or her home. Handful after handful of barbed and bristled, shiny and furry seeds were piled into two Indian baskets that passed from person to person, until they came together at our feet. These seeds were poured into a glass vessel, now kept above the dining room table of our home in the desert.

Every once in a while, I will take that vessel of seeds down from the shelf and rummage through them, remembering plants, places, and friends. "Here is gama grass seed, carried along by Don from the prairies. Here is a Santo Domingo native tobacco pouch, brought back by old Jack from northern New Mexico. There are a few lentils, peas, and *kusa* squash seeds—must be from Lebanese cousins . . ."

Then I see something special and smile. "And look at that Indian corn, that *granoturco*—it looks like it has been here since the beginning!"

Notes

Introduction:
Trekking on Unfamiliar Ground

The discussion of sauntering comes from Henry David Thoreau's interpretation of a nineteenth-century dictionary definition, in "Walking," recently published with an introduction by John Elder, along with Ralph Waldo Emerson's essay "Nature," as *Nature/ Walking* (Boston: Beacon Press, 1991).

Ginger Harmon coauthored with Susanna Margolis a travel guide, *Walking Europe from Top to Bottom* (San Francisco: Sierra Club, 1986).

Yi-fu Tuan's essay "Strangers and Strangeness" appeared in the *Whole Earth Review* 58 (1988).

Carolyn Merchant's *The Death of Nature* (New York: Harper & Row, 1980) remains among the best histories of environmental attitudes in Western intellectual history, although it unfortunately leaves the impression that diverse European ethnic traditions have not persisted in their folk science and sustainable practices that run counter to those of the dominant powers.

Bruce Chatwin's discussion of walking as our evolutionary legacy is in *The Songlines* (New York: Viking Penguin, 1987).

René Dubos discusses why Saint Francis has failed as a saint for ecology in *The Wooing of the Earth* (New York: Charles Scribner's Sons, 1980).

The seminal writings of Alfred Crosby, Jr., on the biological exchanges between the Western and Eastern hemispheres are *The Columbian Exchange* (Westport, Conn.: Greenwood Press, 1972) and *Ecological Imperialism* (Cambridge: Cambridge University Press, 1986).

Chapter 1.
Beyond Columbus: American Tracks
on Mediterranean Soils

Thoreau's "sauntering to the sea" quotation is from his essay "Walking," in *Nature/Walking*, cited in the Introduction.

Kirkpatrick Sale's 1990 revisionist biography of Columbus, *The Conquest of Paradise* (New York: Alfred A. Knopf, 1990), tells much about the man, his misgivings, and his ecological ignorance.

Joy Harjo's quotations come from a short essay called "Field of Miracles," first printed in *Hayden's Ferry Review* (Tempe: Arizona State University Creative Writing Program, summer 1990), no. 6.

Many of the basic patterns of intercontinental crop dispersal and landscape change that occurred in the sixteenth century are discussed by Crosby, McNeill, Hobhouse, and others in an anthology edited by Herman Viola and Carolyn Margolis, *Seeds of Change* (Washington: Smithsonian Institution Press, 1991).

My friend Giuseppe Barbera and his colleagues, Francesco Carimi and Paolo Inglese, summarized *ficodindia* history in "Present and Past Role of the Indian-Fig Prickly Pear (*Opuntia ficus-indica* (L.) Miller, Cactaceae) in the Agriculture of Sicily," *Economic Botany* 46, no. 1 (1992).

The Columbus quotation is found in Sale, *The Conquest of Paradise*.

Aldo Leopold's image of "a world of wounds" comes from his classic, *A Sand County Almanac* (New York: Oxford University Press, 1949).

Lorraine Lilja's description of the Ellis Island scene appeared in "Lost Heritage" in *Gardens for All News* (January–February 1981), the newsmagazine of the National Gardening Association.

Interlude 1.
Leaving Genoa Behind

The epigraph is from Linda Hogan's "Journeys and Other Stories," in *Columbus and Beyond: Views from Native Americans*, edited by Randolph Jorgen (Tucson, Ariz.: Southwest Parks and Monuments Association, 1992).

The discussion of Franciscan influences on Columbus is informed by Kirkpatrick Sale's *The Conquest of Paradise*, cited in Chapter 1, and by a historical investigation by Delno C. West, "Medieval Ideas of Apocalyptic Mission and the Early Franciscans in Mexico," *The Americas* 45, no. 3 (1989).

Fortini's massive treatise on the Assisi of Saint Francis's time is one of the finest attempts I have ever seen to place a historic figure in his cultural, geographic, and social context; see Arnoldo Fortini, *Francis of Assisi*, translated by Helen Moak (New York: Crossroad Publishing, 1982).

Chapter 2.
Florentine Treasures: *Campanilismo* and the Conservers of Local Fruits

This quotation from André Malraux's *Les Voix du Silence* was translated into English by René Dubos and included in his collection of essays, *The Wooing of the Earth*, cited in the Introduction.

The Mark Twain quotation is from *The Innocents Abroad; or, The New Pilgrim's Progress* (New York: Viking Press/Library of America, 1984).

Faith Willinger is an accomplished food writer for magazines in the United States and Italy. I thank her for sharing her knowledge of Signore Torquato with me and for suggesting the visit to the exhibition of Bimbi's paintings.

The history of the tomato presented here is a new synthesis that draws on several reviews of obscure primary materials: Elizabeth Romer's *Italian Pizza and Hearth Breads* (New York: Clarkson N. Potter, 1988); Raymond Sokolov's "The Well-Traveled Tomato," *Natural History*, June 1989; Alan Davidson's "Europeans' Wary Encounter with Tomatoes, Potatoes and Other New World Foods," in N. Foster and L. S. Cordell, eds., *Chilies to Chocolate* (Tucson: University of Arizona Press, 1992); and Mary Simeti's fine *Pomp and Sustenance: Twenty-five Centuries of Sicilian Food* (New York: Henry Holt, 1991).

In 1614, Giacomo Castelvetro described New World beans and squash, likening them to cowpeas and calabashes, respectively, in *The Fruit, Herbs, and Vegetables of Italy*, translated by Gillian Riley (London: Viking Penguin, 1989).

Concerns about European Common Market discouragement of production of heirloom vegetables are discussed in Cary Fowler and Pat Mooney's *Shattering* (Tucson: University of Arizona Press, 1990).

This quotation comes from Archibald Colquhoun's translation of Italo Calvino's fantasy, *Il Barone Rampante*, published in English as *The Baron in the Trees* (New York: Harvest/HBJ Books, 1959).

Bartolomeo Bimbi is featured in Marco Chiarini's *Horticulture as Art: Paintings from the Medici Collections* (Florence: 23rd International Horticultural Congress, 1990) and in Marilena Mosca and Milena Rizotto's *Floralia: Florilegio dalle Collezioni Fiorentine del Sei-Settecento* (Florence: Palazzo Pitti, 1988). A brief biography is included in E. Benezeit's *Dictionnaire Critique et Documentaire des Peintres, Sculpteurs, Dessinateurs et Graveurs* (Paris: Librairie Grund, no date).

The information on Bimbi from the Medici biographer, the eighteenth-century writer Baldinucci, was derived from a mimeographed pamphlet at the Poggio à Caiano villa outside Florence (Florence: 23rd International Horticultural Congress, 1990). See also Chiarini, *Horticulture as Art.*

Giannozzo Pucci annually collects articles about traditional seeds, sustainable agriculture, and alternative economies into a newsletter, *La Fierucola* (Via di Paterno 2, Ontignano 50014, Fiesole, Italy).

The folktale of Saint Francis in his garden at the end of the world came to me via my spiritual guide, Anita Alvarez Williams.

Interlude 2:
Bus Ride to Monte La Verna

Wendell Berry's quip about Americans loathing formality is from his foreword to my book *Enduring Seeds* (San Francisco: North Point Press, 1989).

The quotation from Roxanne Swentzell, a Pueblo Indian sculptor, appeared in the quarterly newsletter of Native Seeds/SEARCH, *The Seedhead News*, summer 1992.

Chapter 3.
La Verna's Wounds: From Montane Sanctuary
to Chestnut Grove

Italo Calvino's 1957 novel, *Il Barone Rampante*, is one of the finest ecological parables ever written and has much to say about forests and human communities. It was translated by Archibald Colquhoun and published in English as *The Baron in the Trees* (cited in Chapter 2).

The story of the welcoming songbirds is from the folk collection called the *Fioretti*, or *Little Flowers of Saint Francis*. This translation is found in Edward A. Armstrong's *Saint Francis: Nature Mystic* (Berkeley: University of California Press, 1973).

Susan Saint Sing's quotation is from her chapbook, *A Pilgrim in Assisi: Searching for Francis Today* (Cincinnati, Ohio: Messenger Press, 1981).

Murray Bodo's view of Francis underground is from *The Way of Saint Francis* (New York: Image/Doubleday, 1985).

J. V. Thirgood's gleanings from historic Italian foresters such as Giuseppe del Noce are included in *Man and the Mediterranean Forest* (New York: Academic Press, 1981).

The chestnut's introduction into Italy is discussed in a technical article by F. Villani and colleagues at the Istituto per l'Agroselvicoltura del CNR in Porano, Italy, "Genetic Variation and Differentiation Between Natural Populations of Chestnut (*Castenea sativa* Mill.) from Italy," in a book edited by H. H. Hattemer and S. Fineschi, *Biochemical Markers in the Population Genetics of Forest Trees* (The Hague: SPB Academic Publishing, 1990). See also their paper "Genetic Differentiation Among Turkish Chestnut (*Castenea sativa* Mill.) Populations," *Heredity* 66 (1991).

Italian chestnut production and blight history are summarized by Lorenzo Mittempergher, "The Present Status of Chestnut Blight in Italy," *Proceedings of the American Chestnut Symposium* (Morgantown: West Virginia University, 1978).

My discussion of chestnut blight is based on articles kindly supplied to me by Sandra Anagnostakis and Jane Cole and on a telephone interview with Dr. Anagnostakis. Key references include her popular pamphlet, *Chestnuts and the Blight* (New Haven: Connecticut Agricultural Experiment Station, 1992), and Aldo Pavari's "Chestnut Blight in Europe," *FAO Newsletter*, 1950.

Elizabeth Romer's classic, *The Tuscan Year: Life and Food in an Italian Valley* (San Francisco: North Point Press, 1989), not only has a detailed recipe for *baldino di castagna* but also stands out as one of the finest books ever written about ethnic food traditions.

Chapter 4.
Sagra di Polenta: Bitter Herbs and the Bread of Poverty

In "Flowery Tuscany," D. H. Lawrence argued that "man *can* live on earth and by the earth without disfiguring the earth. It has been done here [in Tuscany], on all these sculptured hills, and softly, sensitively terraced slopes." This essay was first included in *Phoenix: Posthumous Papers* (New York: Viking Penguin, 1936) and was more recently featured in *The Norton Book of Nature Writing*, edited by Robert Finch and John Elder (New York: W. W. Norton, 1990).

The second epigraph is from Fernand Braudel's *The Structures of Everyday Life: The Limits of the Possible* (New York: Harper & Row, 1979). Much of my discussion of historic changes in population and food production relies on his masterwork, *The Mediterranean and the Mediterranean World in the Age of Philip II*, translated by Sia Reynolds (New York: Harper, 1966), as well as on Jordan Goodman and Katrina Honeymun's *Gainful Pursuits: The Making of Industrial Europe, 1600–1914* (London: Edward Arnold, 1984).

This Lawrence quotation is from "Flowery Tuscany."

The Ovidio Montalbani quotation comes from Piero Camporesi's *Bread of Dreams*, translated by David Gentilcore (Cambridge, Mass.: Polity Press, 1989, distributed by University of Chicago Press).

The Piero Camporesi quotations are from his *Bread of Dreams*.

My research on Italian maize and the rise of pellagra was inspired by a lecture by nutritionist Doris Calloway of the University of California, given at the University of Arizona over a decade ago. Dr. Calloway quoted many unpublished or out-of-print primary documents noted in Paolo Sorcinelli's book about pellagra in central Italy, *Miseria e Malattie nel XIX Secolo* (Milan: Franco Angeli Editore, 1979); Alfred Crosby's *The Columbian Exchange* (cited in the Introduction); Daphne A. Roe's *A Plague of Corn: The Social History of Pellagra* (Ithaca, N.Y.: Cornell University Press, 1973); Elizabeth Etheridge's *The Butterfly Caste* (Westport, Conn.: Greenwood Press,

1972); and Karl Y. Guggenheim's chapter on pellagra in his medical history, *Nutrition and Nutritional Diseases: The Evolution of Concepts* (Lexington, Mass.: Collamore Press, D. C. Heath, 1981).

The Goethe quotation is from Roe's *A Plague of Corn*.

Chapter 5.
Where the Wild Things Aren't: Truffles and Wolves

The quotations from Pierluigi and the other oral histories were taken from the Madonna del Piano elementary school project on truffles, included in *Prima Mostra Mercato del Tartufo Concorso, tra le Scuole, Ricette, Aneddoti, Curiosità e Disegni sul Tartufo* (Perugia/Fabro: Regione dell'Umbria, Giunta Regionale, 1988).

The Lisa Mighetto quotation is from her *Wild Animals and American Environmental Ethics* (Tucson: University of Arizona Press, 1991).

Truffle biology and folklore (including quotations from Sand and others) are covered in Rolf Singer and Bob Harris's *Mushrooms and Truffles: Botany, Cultivation, and Utilization* (Koenigstein: Koeltz Scientific Books, 1987); in the Gruppo Micologico Ternano's *Funghi dell'Umbria* (Terni: Regione dell'Umbria, 1991); and in Ian R. Hall and Gordon Brown's *The Black Truffle: Its History, Uses, and Cultivation* (Mosgiel, New Zealand: Invermay Agricultural Centre, 1988).

Technical information on androstenol is from a 1981 study by Claus and colleagues summarized in Singer and Harris, *Mushrooms and Truffles*, and in Diane Ackerman's *A Natural History of the Senses* (New York: Vintage Books, 1990).

The story of Joseph Talon is from Singer and Harris, *Mushrooms and Truffles*; it is also in Hall and Brown, *The Black Truffle*. Jean Giono's *The Man Who Planted Trees* was most recently published in an edition illustrated by Michael McCurdy (Boston: Chelsea Green, 1988).

Elizabeth Romer's description of a truffle hunter is found in *Italian Pizza and Hearth Breads*, cited in Chapter 2. See also John Haycraft's *Italian Labyrinth: Italy in the 1980s* (London: Secker & Warburg, 1989).

Giacomo Castelvetro's encounter with the German baron is included in the delightful climax to his 1614 manuscript, *The Fruit, Herbs, and Vegetables of Italy*, cited in Chapter 2.

Truffle agroforestry facts are derived from interviews as well as from Lorenzo Mannozzi-Torini's *Manuale di Tartuficoltura* (Rome: Edagricole, no date), *Informazioni, Notizie, Curiosità Micologiche* (Terni: Regione dell'Umbria, Perugia and Gruppo Micologico Terrano, 1988), and from the English texts on truffles already noted.

The best-known version of the legend of the wolf of Gubbio has been disseminated worldwide in the classic *The Little Flowers of Saint Francis*, translated by secular Franciscan Rafael Brown (Garden City, N.J.: Image Books of Doubleday, 1958). Brown includes an appendix that provides circumstantial evidence for a real wolf of Gubbio, tracing the story back as far as 1290. Nevertheless, Edward Armstrong (see the note that follows) has questioned the quality of some of this "factual" evidence and emphasizes the mythical wolf present in medieval minds.

The discussion of lycanthropy is found in Piero Camporesi's *Bread of Dreams*, cited in Chapter 4, and in the Reverend Edward A. Armstrong's analysis of European myth and biological fact, *Saint Francis: Nature Mystic*, cited in Chapter 3. The quotation from Barry Holstun Lopez is from his classic, *Of Wolves and Men* (New York: Charles Scribner's Sons, 1978). Paul Shepard kindly offered a counterpoint to the Lopez thesis, for which I'm grateful.

Professor Luigi Boitani, an eminent zoologist and Species Survival Commission member, discusses the conflicts between men and wolves in his article "Wolf Research and Conservation in Italy," *Biological Conservation*, no. 1 (1992): 125–32.

Interlude 5.
Coming Full Circle

Terry Tempest Williams's comment about the landscape of marriage is paraphrased from her chapbook, *Earthly Messengers* (Salt Lake City, Utah: West Slope Press, 1989).

Chapter 6.
Hands on the Land: Grape Raisers and Bean Eaters

The epigraph is from P. Théophile Desbonnets's *Assisi in the Footsteps of Saint Francis: A Spiritual Guidebook*, translated by Nancy Celashi (Assisi: Edizioni Porziuncola, 1971).

Leonardo Boff, the priest-scholar who has articulated much of the liberation theology that has captured the imaginations of many Latin American Catholics, rejects the view of Saint Francis as a nature mystic and suggests instead that he sought to live with no more power than the poorest of the poor, plant, bird, or human. This quotation is taken from his *Saint Francis: A Model for Human Liberation*, translated by John W. Diercksmeier (New York: Crossroad Publishing, 1985).

D. H. Lawrence is quoted from "Flowery Tuscany," included in Finch and Elder's *The Norton Book of Nature Writing*, cited in Chapter 4.

Much of the discussion on human integration into the Umbrian landscape is informed by the provocative essays of René Dubos in *The Wooing of the Earth*, cited in the Introduction. Depopulation figures for mountain villages come from Francesco Rambotti's *Il Parco del Monte Subasio: Ambiente Fisico e Umano* (Assisi: Accademia Properziana del Subasio, 1986).

The agroecology of the grape-and-hedge-maple association is described by Monica Babetto, M. R. Favretto, M. G. Paoletti, and S. Ragusa of the University of Padua, in their abstract, "3,500 Years' Tradition in Grape (*Vitis vinifera*) and Hedge-Maple (*Acer campestre*)

Association," prepared for the International Conference on Agroecology, Padua, August 1990.

L. W. Hackett's environmental history of malaria remains a classic: *Malaria in Europe: An Ecological Study* (London: Oxford University Press, 1937). For a nontechnical explanation of G6PD deficiency in relation to malaria and favism, I drew on Ann McElroy and Patricia E. Townsend's *Medical Anthropology in Ecological Perspective* (Boulder, Colo.: Westview Press, 1989); and Ronald R. Marquardt's chapter, "Favism," in a volume edited by G. Hawtin and C. Webb, *Fava Bean Improvement* (Wageningen, Netherlands: Marinus Nijhoff Publishers for ICARDA, 1982).

The story of Pythagoras is in Mirko D. Grmek's fascinating chapter regarding fava folklore and medicine, "The Harm in Broad Beans," translated by Mireille and Leonard Muellner for their *Diseases in the Ancient Greek World* (Baltimore, Md.: Johns Hopkins University Press, 1989).

S. H. Katz and J. Schall have published several papers on favism, including "Fava Bean Consumption, G6PD Deficiency, and Malaria," *American Journal of Physical Anthropology* 46 (1977); and the chapter "Favism and Malaria: A Model of Nutrition and Biocultural Evolution" in *Plants Used in Indigenous Medicine and Diet*, edited by N. Etkin (New York: Redgrave Press, 1986). Quotations from Katz come from a 1991 interview with him in Carefree, Arizona, and a recent essay on fava bean coevolution with Mediterranean cultures, still in press.

Interlude 6.
Vendemmia: Bringing in the Vintage

David Price is quoted from his book with photographer Gotthard Schuh, *The Other Italy* (London: Olive Press, 1983).

Ignazio Silone's *Bread and Wine* was in the back of my mind the entire time I was picking grapes, and later, when I was writing; I am partial to his revised version, rewritten nearly twenty years after the first and translated by Eric Mosbacher (London: Guernsey Press for J. M. Dent & Sons, 1986).

Chapter 7.
Feasting on Saint Francis: Animal Rights and the Forgotten Forest of Assisi

The epigraph is from David Price's book with photographer Gotthard Schuh, *The Other Italy*, cited in Interlude 6.

Bert Schwarzchild's story has been assembled from brief interviews with Bert, Marissa Cohen, and Gianfranco Bologna and from the following articles: Bert's "Earthwatch" column, "No Birds Sing on Saint Francis's Mountain," *Audubon* 85, no. 2 (March 1983); Maria Luisa (Marissa) Cohen's conference report, "Assisi: Birthplace of Saint Francis—A New Conservation Park," *The Environmentalist* 5, no. 3 (1985); Marco Ausenda's "San Francisco Contro Assisi," *Airone*, May 1983; and a photocopy of the signed *Dichiarazione del Monte Subasio* from the September 1983 meetings in Assisi.

I am grateful to Lisa Mighetto's work for drawing my attention to William Hornaday's tirades against Italian American hunters. These attacks were published in Hornaday's influential book, *Our Vanishing Wildlife: Its Extermination and Preservation* (New York: New York Zoological Society, 1913); and in his *Wildlife Conservation in Theory and Practice* (New Haven, Conn.: Yale University Press, 1914).

The statistics I cite on hunting in Italy and in Umbria in particular are from an excellent monograph by Piero Belleti and Marco Francone, *La Caccia: Un Sadico e Egoistico Esercizio di Rapina della Fauna* (Turin: Satyagraha Editrice, 1990); and from Rudolf Schreiber's *Save the Birds* (Boston: Houghton Mifflin, 1989).

The Paul Shepard quotation is from a lecture entitled "On Animal Friends," presented at the Woods Hole symposium, "Testing the Biophilia Hypothesis," summer 1992. It will be included in a 1993 Island Press book edited by Stephen Kellert and E. O. Wilson, *The Biophilia Hypothesis.*

The animal rights meeting in Assisi was not the first or the last time I have heard from or read of those who feel it would be better if animals did not kill one another. See, for example, Eric Doyle's *Saint Francis and the Song of Brotherhood* (New York: Seabury Press, 1981).

The quotation from Richard Nelson is slightly paraphrased from his comments at a retreat of nature writers held in honor of John Hay on Cape Cod in September 1991. It represents a theme fully explored in his *The Island Within* (San Francisco: North Point Press, 1989).

The Madge Midley quotation is from her *Beast and Man: The Roots of Human Nature* (Ithaca, N.Y.: Cornell University Press, 1978).

Wendell Berry's "Nature as Measure" is included in *What Are People For?* (San Francisco: North Point Press, 1990).

David Quammen discusses nature within the human gridlock in "A Future as Big as Indonesia" in the special "extinctions" issue of *Left Bank* 2 (Summer 1992).

Epilogue:
Where Did We Go After the Journey?

David Ehrenfeld's essay "Loyalty" first appeared in *Orion* magazine and is included in his collection *Beginning Again: People and Nature in the New Millennium* (New York: Oxford University Press, 1993).

Ignazio Silone's words are spoken by the character Pietro in *Bread and Wine*, cited in Interlude 6.

About the Author

Gary Paul Nabhan grew up in the Indiana Dunes on Lake Michigan among Lebanese relatives. He attended Cornell College and Prescott College, and received his M.S. and Ph.D. from the University of Arizona. He has worked as a plant explorer, teacher in Indian schools and villages, ethnobotanist, seed conservationist, and part-time university professor in botany and creative writing.

Currently, Gary Nabhan is the research director for Native Seeds/SEARCH, writer in residence at the Arizona-Sonora Desert Museum, and a research associate for Conservation International. A recent recipient of a MacArthur Fellowship and a Pew scholarship for conservation research, he is the author of *The Desert Smells Like Rain, Enduring Seeds*, and *Gathering the Desert*. The last was awarded the John Burroughs Medal for nature writing in 1986. In 1991, the Sicilian government awarded Nabhan the Premio Gaia, as one of several artists working toward "a culture of nature."